Praise for *CEO of Me*

"*CEO of Me* takes flexible work arrar  balance to a new level. Employees and employe .."

Paulette Grace, North Am s Leader,
Dow Chemical

"Too many people seek out the primary solution for work life balance from their employer. In reality, balance of work and life requires personal reflection and a personalized solution. *CEO of Me* really hits the mark by focusing the solution in a direction you can control: the mirror."

Lisa Yankie, HR Executive, Financial Services

"*CEO of Me* clearly describes the strategies all of us can use to take control and effectively manage our personal and professional lives. Based on interviews, survey data, and real life (personal and professional) experiences, this book brings definition and clarity to those of us seeking solutions for managing our lives. The book highlights the importance of understanding our values and the important connection between flexibility and commitments. Kossek and Lautsch require us to think more broadly about how we determine our priorities and implement solutions as they provide important value added strategies and their perspectives and insights. Ultimately, this book enables us as individuals to reach our ultimate potential and achieve our goals."

Pamela J Sauter, Senior Vice President, Human Resources,
Qualcomm Incorporated

"*CEO of Me* masterfully blended research-based information with real life case examples to provide practical tools for addressing conflicts between work, family, and life. Authors Kossek and Lautsch have created an exceptionally useful and innovative resource for anyone who wants to achieve a more satisfying balance in their lives."

Michàlle Mor Barak, Ph.D.Professor, School of Social Work
and Marshall School of Business, University of Southern California,
Winner of the Academy of Management Terry Book Award

CEO *of* Me

CEO *of* Me

CREATING A LIFE THAT WORKS IN THE FLEXIBLE JOB AGE

ELLEN ERNST KOSSEK *and* BRENDA A. LAUTSCH

Vice President, Publisher: Tim Moore
Associate Publisher and Director of Marketing: Amy Neidlinger
Wharton Editor: Yoram (Jerry) Wind
Acquisitions Editor: Jennifer Simon
Editorial Assistant: Pamela Boland
Development Editor: Russ Hall
Digital Marketing Manager: Julie Phifer
Marketing Coordinator: Megan Colvin
Cover Designer: Alan Clements
Managing Editor: Gina Kanouse
Project Editor: Chelsey Marti
Copy Editor: Geneil Breeze
Proofreader: San Dee Phillips
Interior Designer: Gloria Schurick
Compositor: Nonie Ratcliff
Manufacturing Buyer: Dan Uhrig

© 2008 by Pearson Education, Inc.
Publishing as Wharton School Publishing
Upper Saddle River, New Jersey 07458

Wharton School Publishing offers excellent discounts on this book when ordered in quantity for bulk purchases or special sales. For more information, please contact U.S. Corporate and Government Sales, 1-800-382-3419, corpsales@pearsontechgroup.com. For sales outside the U.S., please contact International Sales at international@pearsoned.com.

Company and product names mentioned herein are the trademarks or registered trademarks of their respective owners.

Printed in the United States of America

Second Printing February 2008

ISBN-10 0-13-248058-1
ISBN-13 978-0-13-248058-1

Pearson Education LTD.
Pearson Education Australia PTY, Limited.
Pearson Education Singapore, Pte. Ltd.
Pearson Education North Asia, Ltd.
Pearson Education Canada, Ltd.
Pearson Educatión de Mexico, S.A. de C.V.
Pearson Education—Japan
Pearson Education Malaysia, Pte. Ltd.

Library of Congress Cataloging-in-Publication Data is on file.

This product is printed digitally on demand. This book is the paperback version of an original hardcover book.

To the memory of Susan C. Eaton, our friend and thoughtful collaborator

Dr. Susan C. Eaton, an assistant professor at the J. F. Kennedy School at Harvard University, passed away in December 2003. Prior to her death, we had spent several years working intently with Susan collecting data and writing on some early ideas related to this project. We miss the wisdom and warmth she added to this research and our lives.

Contents

Acknowledgments

We would like to thank Jen Simon of Pearson Education for all her patience and help in shaping our message for the real world. We thank Russ Hall for editorial help, The School of Labor & Industrial Relations at Michigan State University for providing several graduate assistantships that helped with data collection, and the companies we studied for providing access and research support. We also thank our families and work colleagues for their continued support while we spent many hours focusing our energy and attention toward the writing of the book.

About the Authors

ELLEN ERNST KOSSEK, professor at Michigan State University's School of Labor & Industrial Relations (Ph.D. Yale), is a leading expert on research on improving relationships between work, family, and personal life in organizations, new ways of working related to flexibility (telecommuting, flextime, reduced-load work), management of talent and diversity in the global multicultural firm, and workplace innovation and change. She has published dozens of articles and a number of books on these topics. She was elected to the Board of Governors of the National Academy of Management, chair of the Gender and Diversity in Organizations Division, and fellow of American Psychological Association and Society of Industrial Organizational Psychology. Her research on work and personal life has been supported by the Alfred P. Sloan Foundation, the National Institute of Occupational Safety and Health, the Gerber Foundation, and major corporations. She has taught managers in North America, Europe, and Asia. She is married with four children.

BRENDA A. LAUTSCH, associate professor at Simon Fraser University in Canada, received her Ph.D. in industrial relations and human resources management from The MIT Sloan School of Management. Her research examines the equity and work-life implications of new ways of working, including contingent and flexible work forms. Her work appears in leading journals such as the *Industrial and Labor Relations Review*, the *Journal of Vocational Behavior*, and *Industrial Relations*. She is married with two delightful sons (Oscar age 4 and Kaspar age 7 months).

Preface

If I'm such a success, why isn't my life feeling more manageable? If my life is so ideal on paper, why do I still have this nagging concern that relationships between work and home could be improved for the better? I know I can make some changes to improve things, but I just keep doing things the same old way.

Dan, 31, sales manager with a five year old

If you have asked yourself a question similar to this one you're not alone. Today, many accomplished individuals still feel dissatisfied with the quality of their lives. Building a life that works better for you on and off the job means believing that you are the CEO of your life starting today. This will enable you to create a better working life and make changes—many often small and simple—that will enable you to gain more control over how you manage your many commitments, at work and at home. You will understand by reading this book the new rules for managing work and personal life, the first and foremost being that we are the masters and mistresses of our fate. We can make better choices; we are not subject to the whims of our overcommitted schedules, and the laptops and cell phones that allow us to work anywhere, anyplace, and any time. We will provide you a new way of thinking and a framework so that you can learn how to make better choices to make your life better.

Like many working individuals, you always strive to do well in your job, take care of your home, and achieve a satisfying personal life. But how? Lately does it seem like your personal and work life are colliding more and more? Sure, most of us have the flexibility to check e-mail at home as we let the dog out or get the kids ready for school. We are used to calling our boss in the car while commuting and text messaging our next appointment—it's a given that the nature of work in our daily life has changed. We live in a world with increased blurring between work and home, which we believe enables us to make our life better and find balance. Most of us have simply too much to do in too little time, and technology helps us to virtually be in two places at the same time. But could this increased flexibility to mix our jobs and our nonwork interests also have the potential to screw things up?

Granted, many of us don't mind multitasking—doing work, personal, and family tasks all at the same time. But, do you ever wonder whether it really is good for our personal relationships to be taking cell phone calls during the weekends, vacations, and dinner? Are we really giving our best when we switch back and forth between our coworkers and instant messaging with family and friends? Is it good for our health and well-being to be checking work e-mail right up to bedtime while watching TV in our bedroom as we are getting ready to doze off to sleep?

To be effective "whole people"—people who really excel on the job and at home—it is vital to understand the new rules for work and life that make us increasingly the CEOs of our own lives. Sure, there's a lot of noise out there in the media on the need for work-life balance and how to do it, but it's not going to be useful to you unless you first understand how you are currently using flexibility in your life and whether how you are using it makes your life better or worse. The key that we found that we want to share with you—and that is the big idea of this book—is as CEO of your life, *you can take control of your life to make flexibility work for you instead of against you.* To do this, you must understand your *flexstyle*—how you manage the physical and psychological mixing of work and personal life. Then and only then can you learn how to make changes to ensure you use flexibility to help rather than hurt your life. Otherwise, too much flexibility leads to overlapping of work and personal life in ways that make us unhappy. And with the way society and technology have changed to enable more and more mixing between the two in our 24/7 wired world, unless we actively manage how we use flexibility, the flexibility that was supposed to help us can actually make our lives worse.

But as CEO of your life, you have the choice to avoid the flexibility trap. You can learn how to use flexibility to make your life better. You can begin by understanding your flexstyle, which is how you are currently managing relationships between work and personal life, your style for creating a workable life. You also should take stock of how well your flexstyle fits with the people you live and work with. You need to know what's working and what's not working so well and how to make changes—sometimes small and sometimes more drastic—to shift where you draw the line between work and non-work to be more effective on the job and at home.

This is the goal of this book: to help you better understand how you are currently managing relationships between work and personal life; identify gaps in how well it fits with your actual values, jobs, and family and personal life; and determine what actions you can take to make changes and negotiate a new deal that works better. This will enable you to close the gap between your values and dreams and how you are currently living your life to have more satisfying relationships with your family and friends, customers, bosses, coworkers, and even your own personal identity. This book will help you find a better way to manage your work and personal life, regardless of where you work and who you are, and offers you a new framework for making better choices.

By reading this book you will be able to

- Learn how to take charge of your life to implement new ways for using flexibility to make life work better.

- Better evaluate the different choices you make, either consciously or unconsciously, that shape how your work and personal life fit together.

- Develop more positive relationships between your work and personal life

- Get practical diagnostic tools and self-assessments to determine how you are currently using flexibility in your working life and how it may be getting in the way of the life that you really want.

- Identify the barriers that block you from making true personal changes.

- Get practical tips and tools for making changes.

- Identify which of the three flexstyle types you use to manage work and life relationships and determine whether you use flexibility to make your life better or worse. By finding your flexstyle, you will discover whether you're a Captive or a Work or Family Firster, a Fusion Lover or a Reactor, a Job Warrior or a Quality Timer.

- Learn tips and tools that you can use to improve the quality of your working life.

- Find strategies that work to negotiate a better deal (based on leading negotiation principles) that consider the interests of other parties, such as your bosses, coworkers, and family, who are invested in how you are currently managing work and personal life relationships to develop win-win solutions to work and life conflicts.

- Learn how to make it easier for you and the people you work and live with to have more effective working and personal lives.

- Get a refreshing new spin on the work-life dilemma.

- Make better choices and create a life that works on your terms.

Although work-life balance is an age-old problem, until now no book has offered as innovative or as useful solutions as this one does that anyone can use.

About the Research on Which This Book Was Based

The ideas behind *CEO of Me* started with a study of literally hundreds of professionals and managers with varying levels of access to flexible work arrangements in four different types of organizations in North America. Several years ago, we started studying telecommuting, new ways of working, and the use of formal flexible work arrangements using scientific methods of control groups in naturally occurring organizational experiments.

We wanted to present examples of varieties of ways people work today. One set of surveys and interviews was collected from individuals who worked for a large manufacturing organization and who had limited access to flexible working arrangements. We wanted to include employees from a manufacturing environment, a context that typically has been excluded from most work-family flexibility studies. We were surprised to find that even individuals with limited access to flexibility found different ways of crafting workable lives. Another set of surveys and interviews was conducted with individuals who worked at either a major global financial services firm (pseudonym of Infocom) or a major computer company (pseudonym of Datacorp), and who sometimes worked at home or virtually either on nights or weekends by choice or a day or more a week. A third set of interviews was conducted with people at these firms who never or rarely worked at home or virtually.

The fourth set of interviews was conducted with high talent individuals (mostly women) who left mainstream corporate life when they had growing families. Some of these interviews were conducted with highly successful individuals who left a major revered Fortune 100 employer often on the 100 Best companies list to start their own, now thriving, consulting firm. Ironically, they now often serve as vendors to their former employer. Others we interviewed had less high powered jobs but still were successfully working for pay and managing caregiving. This fourth group is essentially part of what the popular media calls the "opting out" group—women who opt out of corporate American when they find the challenges of managing work and family too demanding in current corporate environments. It was our view that workplace studies tend to ignore the people who leave Corporate America. Yet to change Corporate America, we need to understand why some people left. Sometimes those who leave are studied on their own, such as in opting out research, but rarely are they included as part of a study that looks at use of workplace flexibility and managing career and personal life. Individuals who opt out are sometimes treated in the work-family literature as though they do not have careers or work-family conflict. We include them in the study as well because they are part of the story of the different ways people strive to create a better working life. An overview of our research methods and continuing research on how to create effective work-life relationships is found in the appendix.

We include numerous detailed cases throughout the book to illustrate different ways of working and of meshing work and personal life. As we do so, we use pseudonyms for both organizations and individuals. Details of the stories of the individuals we studied and include in the book are disguised—sometimes dramatically—to preserve confidentiality and to protect their privacy. We also drew on the culmination of our team's combined more than 30 years of research on work and family and flexibility. In addition, our experiences as professional women struggling with that elusive (and often problematic) term *work-family balance* in our own lives, helped us to understand the daily struggles of our informants to cope with work, kids, health crises, and self- and elder-care, and informed the writing of this book.

We found that it didn't matter so much whether a person was a formal telecommuter or a user of work-life policies. It also didn't matter the type of family a person had or the gender, occupation, or type of company a person worked for. Rather what mattered most was how individuals self-managed relationships between work and home and how they *felt* about the way they were living their lives and managing their work-life relationships—what we label in this book as *flexstyles*. Two people can be doing exactly the same thing, such as telecommuting and leaving the baby with a sitter in the next room, and one person can feel great about it, and the other can feel unhappy and in pain.

So like us, you may have read some of the books out there already that propose their own solutions to the kind of work-life issues you are dealing with and come away unsatisfied. Mainstream and academic writers highlight a scant list of options: You must either revamp the entire organization in which you work to improve things (a daunting task for most), leave the organization, or do nothing and put up with the status quo. This book instead offers practical options of different ways to manage work and family relationships to create a better working life. We propose changes to the ways you are combining work and personal life demands so that you can tailor a unique situation to fit your needs. This personal journey of self-improvement is especially important until societal and employer support to help all employees manage the work-life interface becomes widespread and not the exception.

This book will allow you to understand what you are currently doing as CEO of your life, to reflect on what's working well and not so well in light of what's most important to you and those you live and work with, and then to make practical changes to ensure your life is constructed around those priorities. You will come away with a life that works—on your terms!

chapter one

Are You the CEO of Your Working Life?

Life is a constant balancing act. There is always something that happens for which one cannot plan. It helps to have some flexibility, but my new supervisor is not very supportive of personal issues so we are trying to work things out. I'm not a compartmentalized person where I can just shut off one thing. My family and work go where I do so it is a package deal. It's hard to put one over the other. You need a good support system and a good manager.

Dylan, Account Manager, Datel, a major computer services firm

Do You Want to Change How You Are Balancing Work and Personal Life?

I remember feeling like I had only one thing in my life—work. I remember feeling a little sad all the time, like something was missing in my life, and I was really getting burnt out. Yes, I truly enjoy my job and am really good at what I do, but I realized my days were taken up with work, errands, chores, and sleep and that's about it. I hate how I am living.

Mary, single school teacher in her late twenties

Mary teaches seventh grade in Tucson. Looking back on the last several years as she began her teaching career, she remembered feeling so pressured to keep up at work that she hadn't had the time to take a vacation in years. Although her teaching job pays her for only nine months, and she has the summers off, her life year-round is filled with school projects, e-mail and conferences. She was almost ready to quit when she finally got up the courage to talk to her principal at school about how unhappy she was with her life.

The principal was totally caught off guard. Mary was one of his best employees, and he would have hated to lose her. He jumped into action to help Mary and made sure she was the first to get a teaching intern in the fall to help dramatically reduce her workload. He also gave Mary "permission" to take a year sabbatical from all extra school committees. Mary had served on more committees than any of her peers in her five years teaching at the school; it was time for someone else to step up to the plate or a wonderful employee would be burned out and lost. Mary learned that she needed to have the courage to start making life change just by speaking up and asking. She also learned she didn't have to always do it all. She gave herself permission to cut back a little at work. The light bulb went on! She realized she didn't have to keep up this pattern of overachievement she had been socialized into her entire life. No one was forcing her to burn herself out. By taking this small step toward change, she learned she could find her love of work again and take better care of herself.[1]

> *I do the chores as I need to do throughout the day when I am able to work from home. I believe being able to work from home sometimes benefits my family because I can take time out for children and work later at night when they are in bed. One day, I might work 9:00 a.m. to 1:00 p.m., go play golf or go to a matinee, and then work from 8:00 a.m. through 11:00 p.m. a couple other days to make up the time. It's a great working arrangement. My job is very flexible. I can organize my workday how I want it and be able to spend some time with my family. As long as I get my job done, my employer doesn't care. Everybody works this way in my company— it's no big deal—it's part of our culture.*
>
> *Rick, "40 something" technology consulting professional at Infocom, a major information services firm*

Rick is married with two school-age children. He has a master's degree from a prestigious graduate school and has worked for eight years at his firm. His "office" is either at the customer site or out of his home. Yes, it's sometimes hard when he travels a lot, and it can get a little hectic keeping up his home office. And sometimes the neighbors and kids get confused about when he is working, but he wouldn't have it any other way. He purposely sought out a job with Infocom (pseudonym), his employer, because he knew about its culture of flexibility. Infocom's philosophy is that a company doesn't manage people's working time by the clock but by how much they can manage themselves effectively to get their jobs done. Output is what matters for performance, and Rick works well in this kind of culture. At the time Rick took this job, all his friends were going to much more prestigious firms and making a lot more money. Rick knew that having some time for his family was important to him and his wife. Now he smiles a little to himself when many of his friends ask his advice on how he does it. They want to do it, too—find better balance and more meaning in how they put together their work and personal life.

At the end of each day, I give myself a report card on how I did today. I ask myself, "Do I feel like I was a good mom, wife, and employee today? Did I refrain from yelling at anyone today at work or home? Did I give my best to my kids and spouse as I intended AND at the same time did I get everything done today that I promised my boss and clients?"

Robin, 30-year-old former business analyst
at a high technology firm who left to become a freelance reporter

---

Robin made this life change to become a freelance reporter after she felt things weren't working for her and her family when she was working in her old corporate job. She looked back on how frustrated she had felt before changing careers to make her life work better. "I felt like my generation was sold a raw deal—a bill of goods on managing career and family. We were told we could 'have it all.' I was working for a manufacturing firm. I thought this was a progressive company. We had a lot of flexibility available to us, like flextime and the ability to work from home. But you know what? I was constantly writing proposals at midnight. I thought, 'What is wrong with this picture?' It was too much. So I took my skill at writing and changed occupations. I left corporate life to freelance from home. I am now very deliberate and organized in my work after the kids leave for school. Yes, one downside is I make less money, but I am much happier, and things are working much better for my family, too. I feel great that I had the guts to make this change before my old office peers did—the ones I saw lose their jobs about a year and a half after I quit. I also am happy I didn't stop working. We need the money and couldn't live the way we like on one income, and I love my job. I also love being able to go to the gym and exercise several times a week; I even joined a book club—something I never could find time to do when I was working so many hours and commuting so much."

Are you unhappy with the way your personal life is meshing with your work life, and would you like to find better choices to create a better working life? Would you like to draw the lines differently between your work, family, and personal life? Are you dissatisfied with how you are allocating your energy and time in your life—that you're not giving your best self to your family, your job, or even yourself? Do you have ongoing conflicts over the work-life balance choices you have made? Or do you believe you can't change things to create better options because of constraints you feel you can't control? Maybe you've even had your family or friends or coworkers tell you more often than you'd like that you need to manage your job and personal life relationships differently? Maybe someone even bought this book for you.

You are not alone. Many people today feel like the different parts of their lives—their jobs, their families, their time for themselves—are often at odds, and there is nothing they can do about it. Like them, you wish you could make a change. Besides changing yourself, you also want others in your life—your family, your friends, or your boss—to give you the support you need so that you can be successful in making changes. You need the key people in your world to relate to you in new ways that can help you create healthier relationships between all the important balls you juggle in your life. You might be frustrated with the formal solutions currently available—such as your company's flexible work schedules, which are supposed to help with work-life balance—at least on paper. But perhaps your boss doesn't like you to use these policies; or even when you do use them, you find you still have a lot of work-life conflicts.

You Are the CEO of Your Life Starting Today!

To help you address these questions, *CEO of Me* is based on a simple idea that is brought to life in the three stories of change that Mary, Rick, and Robin—the individuals you met at the beginning of this chapter—made in their approaches to putting together their work and personal lives. In each of these stories, the individuals adopted some new beliefs and actions that helped them take steps to make their "life work better." In essence, the central idea they bought into, which you can too, is this: You are the CEO of your life—starting today! When you accept this belief, you will be able to apply some simple rationales to help you come to a better choice on how to make it all work together. We will share with you some of the new rules of making life work better to help you make changes. We start with explaining the logic of what we have just shared.

You Probably Have More Choice Than You Think to Take Further Control of How You Manage Work and Personal Life Relationships

This first rule is built on the recognition that you must see yourself in the driver's seat in charge of your life. Perhaps you have never thought about your personal life as something you need to actively lead and manage like a CEO does, but to make significant life change, you should! In the business world, a CEO is the chief executive officer who is in charge of the management of the entire corporation. The CEO makes strategic choices that deeply affect the organization's current and future health. As CEO of your own life, you constantly make choices about how to manage your work and life, whether you recognize it or not. So, you have more choice than you think in how you can make work and life work. You *do* have the power to create more work-life choices. After you accept that you are the master or mistress of your working life and fate, you will be able to make better choices. You will see you are not subject to the whims of your overcommitted schedule. You will begin to understand a new way of thinking and a framework for making choices.

This leads us to the next key rule, or fact, that facilitates your ability to make a change like the individuals in the beginning of this chapter.

You Can Create a Better Employment Deal Because of the New Flexible Job Age

A second reason you can be the CEO of your life, starting today, is that we are in an unprecedented era of flexible work options. This new age of flexibility is based on several main facts that have transpired over the last 20 to 30 years in the employment setting. Even if these facts are not yet transpiring at your particular employer, they seem to be here to stay. Awareness of these labor market changes will help you to bargain better and visualize a new deal.

The first fact is the transformed *psychological contract* of careers and jobs in general.[2] There is greater acceptance of more variation and diversity in employment deals. Whether you have ever heard this term, it is an age-old one in the organizational psychological and management literatures. We all have a psychological contract with our employers—this is the unwritten beliefs our employer and we have about our commitments toward each other. It is basically what are the appropriate relationships and implicit deals we cut with each other regarding loyalty and treatment, and it has indeed changed to see flexibility increasingly as a two-way street.

More than at any time in recent history, employers are seeking more flexibility in the employment relationship. They are no longer looking to offer you a lifelong career. For example, your job security is only as good as your last quarter's performance and how your labor costs and skills match up on the global market. There can be no more coasting at any point in your career either. Your pension benefits are increasingly portable, too. This gives you the flexibility and option to move between workplaces more than in the past. As for sticking with your employer for health-care benefits—forget it. Even that is being eroded for many of us as our health-care co-payments increase and retirement benefits are cut. If you are a U.S. employee working for a large employer with group-based health-care plans, your health-care coverage might be one where you are covered for up to three years if you do change employers, under COBRA—a U.S. group-based health-care benefits law—to ensure some health-care benefits if you change employers or lose your job.

What does this mean for you in terms of managing your work and life? Don't count on the employer to take care of you or make decisions for you over a 30-year career like your parents or grandparents might have experienced. The idea of a long career with one employer is in the past: You must manage your career and life decisions, take care of yourself, and actively manage your decisions to create the life that you want.

This leads to another major fact enabling each of us to be the "CEO of Me"—to create more choice to make life work better. You have greater opportunity for access to flexible work arrangements in the employment setting than ever before. Whether it has arrived at your employer, more and more companies offer many kinds of flexibility policies in work schedules, hours, and locations. Perhaps you have *flextime*—the ability to start and stop working time when you want—or *telecommuting*—the ability to work from home. Or you can work *part-time* or with *reduced load work* options, take *sabbaticals* and *leaves-of-absence*. Maybe you work *compressed work weeks* of four 10-hour days or 80 hours over two weeks. Or you have the ability to *use intermittent sick time and family and personal leaves* such as in the United States for personal, medical, or care-giving needs not just for yourself but for your family or pet. These are just some of the many options available. If you don't have these at your company, you need to ask for them or think about moving to an employer that does offer them.

Your Workplace is Shifting Toward Growing Acceptance of Different Types of Families and Work Schedules

The third fact contributing to the ability to be the CEO of your life is that there is growing widespread acceptance of different types of families and personal living arrangements. The workplace is shifting to recognize that employees come to work with a wide variety of different family types influencing identities and work schedules. While, certainly, some barriers exist in terms of embracing so-called "nontraditional families and ways of working," we are fortunate that truly on a national and international scale there is greater acceptance of these situations. We might be gay or straight. We might choose to never marry, or we might divorce or remarry. Perhaps we are dual earner or dual career couples, maybe even with a stay-at-home dad and a working mom as the primary breadwinner. Or we might be *sandwiched-generation families*, where we care for our kids in school and our aging parents all at the same time as we are employed. For some, college kids might return and live at home as they start their careers to save money against skyrocketing housing costs. Some might choose to never have kids even if married. Others might not be married but choose to adopt as a single parent. Or some of us are elderly individuals who retire from one career and then turn around and "unretire" for a second career.

This slow growing acceptance of different types of families and employees and different ways of working is because the workforce in the United States in particular has transformed in terms of changing demographics. The census bureau reports that more than 83% of all families with two parents and kids at home have dual earners.[3] More and more people are living as single persons than at any time in U.S. history. Fifty percent of all people surveyed at major corporations, who are age 50 or over, stated they would like to work part-time on the way to retirement and maybe even never retire. Nearly 40% of all professionals and managers at major U.S. companies are women—many with significant nonwork responsibilities. The growing diversity of the U.S. workforce and the global labor market shift toward offshoring has also created more change options for us. When we work with people of different cultures, we find out that we must respect different national holidays, set phone calls for work at different times in the 24/7 global clock, and respect different cultural values about how work and personal life should be meshed—including simple things such as accompanying a wife to the doctor for a prenatal visit.

We also ask our employers to respect a greater diversity of geographies in our primary residences, longer commutes, and to change cultures to adopt new face time rules and ways of assessing performance. The notion of all employees in the same community working for the same employer under the same hours and direct supervision in a company town is becoming rarer and rarer. The Internet and ability to work at a distance from the main workplace enables us to live in one town and work in another several hours or many time zones away by airplane.

Take Laurel, the vice president of a bio tech company in Iowa who one author of this book recently met on a plane. She lives and telecommutes in

Charlotte, North Carolina, two weeks a month where her husband is a stay-at-home dad caring for the kids ages five and seven. The other two weeks she works intently onsite for her biotech employer in Iowa. She was able to negotiate this deal with her employer because she is talented and makes sure her work doesn't get behind when she is offsite. Her family did not want to move to Iowa, and this has enabled her to keep a happy household. She likes to focus intently on work when she is at corporate for two weeks at a time, and then she re-enters her family's geography when she is telecommuting from home during her offsite work weeks.

Employers like Laurel's have finally woken up to the fact that this growing diversity in the workforce and in families means that not all ideal employees work the same way, work the same hours, and work in the same location. There is budding acceptance of different employment deals to meet different types of families and the personal needs of workers. When you believe you have the choice to make a change and you become aware of the growing acceptance of different employment deals—maybe not at your current employer but across the spectrum of leading employers—it becomes possible for you to see and act on these choices.

You Can Adopt New Language and Images for Talking About Work and Life Issues to Enable You to Think Differently About the Options Available

We propose the term *flexstyle* as a new way to think about your approach to how you manage flexibility between work and life to make them fit together on a day-to-day basis. In the following chapters, we tell you more about what flexstyle is—but, in a nutshell, it is how you manage actions, emotions, and thoughts to create a pattern combining work and personal life that generally makes you feel happy, or not so happy, about your working life. To make a change, it is important to start thinking about your work-life balance in a new way. Move away from the notion in popular culture of managing work and personal life as a balancing act—like juggling, walking a tightrope in the circus, or balancing weights on a fulcrum scale. This mental model gets in the way of helping you see new possibilities about how to make a change, because rarely are your different life threads—your career, family, and personal strands—blended equally in a coordinated tapestry. Life is not a puzzle where all pieces fit neatly, or an orchestra where all instruments are synchronized in perfect harmony. A picture of a perfectly balanced life is one few of us can ever achieve at any single point in time.

Sure, the term *balance* is used a lot in the popular press, and your boss or partner knows what you mean when you talk about needing more of it. But don't let yourself be misled by the term. Don't assume that everyone balances work and family equally or wants things to be on an even plane—or even has a personal or job situation that lets them try to achieve this. This "perfect balance" image also sets up confusion about the different parts of what makes us who we are— our identities that make up the many threads of our life tapestry. We see ourselves as a family member, as a person with a career and interesting job, or as someone who takes the time to solve a community problem or visit an ill friend, and whatever else we do for fun to complete our whole being, from exercising and playing golf to volunteering at church. It makes these identities seem at odds, in a negative win-lose relationship where these things are at war with each other. Images that are at odds can lead us to see our choices as in an either-or world that might not fully reflect our reality.

Take the age old debate about whether women should quit working when they have young children. As Leslie Bennetts states in her 2007 book, *The Feminine Mistake*, for women to depend on their spouses for all livelihood, to chose to be a stay at home mother when one would rather work is not just a lifestyle choice but is a dire economic choice that can make it exceedingly diffi-cult for many women to return to the workforce. The other images of the career driven supermom in the popular media aren't all that helpful or reflective of real-ity either. These images and notion of perfect "balance" can create difficulties, because it implies that we all want to or can give equal weight to the work and nonwork dimensions of our lives—which isn't accurate.

Moreover, people prioritize the work and nonwork aspects of their lives dif-ferently as their lives progress. Though someone might give the different dimen-sions equal priority at one point in his life, the balance might change at a later point; for example, with the birth of a child, job promotion, or some other major shift. Also, people's starting points in the marathon of making decisions over how to manage jobs and personal relationships are not identical and placed in two bal-anced baskets. If you are a single parent, you come to the table with a different set of resources and needs than someone with a stay-at-home partner. If you work for a manager or a company that is sympathetic to your personal needs, you have more choices and options to create how you manage work and personal life. Thus, managing work and life demands is rarely perfectly balanced evenly on a scale, nor is it perfectly at odds. For example, the term *work-family conflict* cre-ates problems because it immediately sets up an image of work and family as being in a win-lose competition in the battle for our time, energy, and life resources. Using work and family in juxtaposed language also creates problems by suggesting that only people with visible families and care-giving demands can have tensions over where they "draw the line" to demarcate work and personal life. Some pundits came up with the new phrase *work-life* as a means to address this and to suggest that all employees, even those without a family, can have stress in meshing work and personal life. Even the phrase "work and life" or "work versus life" causes concern, because it implies that they are two different things. Work *is* a part of life, just as family, community, and personal responsibilities are parts of life.

The commonly used phrases *work and life integration* or *work and life separation* likewise pose problems for some people. Neither blending work and non-work nor keeping them compartmentalized from one another is an ideal approach for every employee. So get away from the outdated language of balance and conflict.

Think in Terms of Flexstyles: How Might You Use Flexibility More Effectively to Create More Positive Relationships Between Work and Personal Life?

How do we talk about the challenge of achieving lives that are fulfilling and meaningful on all fronts? How do we avoid overused and downright inaccurate language, or words that have very different meanings to different people?

In this book, when we use the term *flexstyle* as a way of thinking about how to create more healthy relationships between work and personal life, we want you to stop thinking about work and family and work and life problems as an issue of balance or imbalance. Instead, start thinking about how you can more effectively use flexibility to navigate and manage relationships between work and personal life in ways that work better for you. This new way of thinking will give you new tools and ways to think and talk about work-life issues.

The first step in making a change is to start thinking about having *positive* relationships between work and personal life that make you feel good about both at the same time. When this happens, you don't feel you are making too many sacrifices at work that get in the way of meeting your personal life dreams and day-to-day needs. Conversely, you don't feel like you are hurting your job or giving up on your career dreams to "have a life" and take care of your family or personal needs. You have a new vision of what your life could be if things were to fit together in more healthy relationships. This way of thinking enables you to conceive new possibilities to challenge what you are currently doing to move closer toward your dream way of living.

To Make a Change, Begin Your Self-Reflective Journey by Conducting a "Life Bucket Analysis"

You should reflect on whether you are currently investing your time and energy on what matters most to you. Understanding your current level of satisfaction with where you are currently allocating your time and energy is a valuable tool to help you determine whether you want or need to change how you are "drawing the line" to make up the pieces of the total pie representing your life pursuits. Using this tool, you consider how well you're allocating your time and energy to the roles and responsibilities most important to you. This exercise builds on the notion that devoting more of your time and energy to those roles you identify with and care most about should be a guiding principle for how you are managing work and personal life relationships. You need to challenge yourself to think about how you are currently investing your time and energy and to what extent these investments reflect your true priorities.

Instructions:

1. Think about how you spend your time and energy in a typical week. There are 168 hours in a week. In creating pie slices or life buckets to represent dimensions of your life, consider your career, family, friends, personal pursuits and well-being, community obligations, social activism, and any other commitments that strike you as important If you separate your time into buckets, it might look something like Figure 1.1.

Figure 1.1 *Separating pieces of your life into buckets.*

You can also envision these life buckets as a pie chart by drawing a large circle to represent your different life buckets—how you see the pieces of your life fitting together to make up a pie. Divide this "pie" into segments representing the major work and nonwork dimensions of your life—and the amount of time and energy you devote to each. For example, if you invest one half of these resources in your job, one quarter of them in your family, and another quarter in personal interests (such as exercise, spiritual reflection or religion, volunteer work, and relaxation), your circle would look like the one shown in Figure 1.2. Be honest: Show your *actual* allocations of time and energy to the different dimensions—not what you think your allocations *should* be. With the aforementioned guidelines in mind, draw your pie chart next the example.

DRAWING LIFE BUCKETS

How am I currently spending my time and energy?

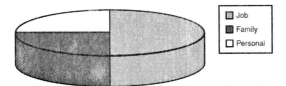

Figure 1.2 *Drawing my current life buckets.*

2. Draw another large circle, this time showing how you would *like* to allocate your time and energy to the different dimensions in your life. If you could make changes to allocate your time and energy differently to fit with your vision and values of how you would really like to live your life, what would the pie look like (see Figure 1.3)? Draw your *new* pie with different life allocations next to the example.

DRAWING NEW LIFE BUCKETS

What are my dreams for how I would like to spend my time and energy?

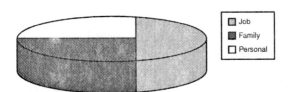

Figure 1.3 *Visioning new life buckets.*

3. Compare the two circles. To what extent are you allocating your time and energy in congruence with what you value most? Which dimensions of your life are most out of alignment? For example, are there commitments to which you want to devote a significant percentage of your time and energy, but you're actually investing only a small percentage in these dimensions of your life?

4. Ask yourself whether any of the misalignments you've identified stem from how you are currently managing your life. For example, in what ways is how you are currently using flexibility to manage work and personal life interactions, contributing to this mismatch? If you're allocating more time and energy to your career than you would prefer, is this because you are letting clients and coworkers call you at home during evenings and weekends and allowing your job to overshadow how you are spending your personal time?

Any type of mismatch means that you are devoting valuable time and energy to a role that is less close to your main values. You might live with this mismatch in the short term, but in the longer term, you will likely feel increasingly dissatisfied. As you'll see, changing your flexstyle can help correct mismatches related to how you manage your work, personal time, family, and other commitments.

In this chapter, you have taken the first step toward implementing some of the new rules to make your life work better. Start by believing you have more choice than you think in how you can use flexibility to create a better quality working life. As the CEO of your life, you can make changes. You begin to understand how you are allocating your time and energy across your life buckets and how you are managing work and life relationships. We can be sometimes our own worst enemy in creating our own work-life conflicts by not understanding how we are physically and psychologically mixing work and family and the tradeoffs we have and our life context. In the rest of the book, we give you a framework for making new decisions to make your life work better. We have found that making small changes sometimes produces extraordinary results.

> **I don't wish I could spend more time at the office. I had a heart attack scare that put things into perspective for me. I realized things needed to change.**
>
> Bob, 50-year-old male who worked more than 60 hours a week for years for an information technology company

That is another main message we revisit throughout the book—how to make small changes to use the new flexibility between work and non-work to make your life work much better.

Why Change Is Tough

Maybe you have tried to make changes on how you manage work and personal life relationships in the past but haven't been successful. If this is the case, you are like many people we interviewed. Making true change is hard. We would be guilty of talking about making life changes too easy if we weren't up front with you on this. Here are some of the reasons why you might have tried to make changes in the past but found you couldn't make it happen.

Why Changing How You Manage Work-Life Relationships Is Hard

- You have a lack of control (real or perceived) over work and family demands and are unsure how to gain control.
- You have not garnered social and tangible resources from key partners at work and home to help you make changes.
- You have not figured out how to negotiate with key stakeholders and frame arguments on how supporting change will serve their interests, too.
- You find it easier and more efficient in the short run to stick to old habits.
- You are so overworked and overwhelmed that making changes feels like one more job.
- You cannot envision any other way of living better because you haven't tried it.
- You don't see any new choices or don't want to "rock the boat."
- You do not realize that not trying to make a change is in fact a choice.
- You are unwilling to make tradeoffs involved in moving to a new way of living and managing your life.

- You are addicted to work and find the immediate feedback from work easier than dealing with the messy stuff in your personal life.
- You think that drastic change is the only solution and this results in paralysis and inertia.
- You don't understand that change is an iterative cycle, and you need to experiment with change as part of the change process.

Don't forget that change is part of a cycle. People often have to engage in trial and error and get feedback on new ways of working as they move toward a solution. It's difficult to fully appreciate all the pros and cons of a particular approach until you live it, and so it's common to have to make a series of changes. Professor Herminia Ibarra of INSEAD found this out when she studied people who successfully changed careers.[4] She found that experimenting with changes was how people successfully managed to make a big life change. The same wisdom applies to making a change in our personal work and family dynamics. We need to not be afraid to experiment and learn from our mistakes. It takes trial and error and a commitment to learn from feedback of each incident we try to manage.

And most importantly, we cannot change something we do not understand. We must first assess the dynamics of how we are currently managing work and personal life. This is understanding the concept of flexstyles. As you start this journey toward becoming the CEO of your life, in the next chapter you will explore and begin to understand flexstyles and discover your own.

chapter two

Knowing Your Flexstyle

> *I don't really have big walls around either of them (work and family).*
> *If something big is going on, one tends to bleed over into the other.*
> *That's just the way my life is.*
>
> "Haley," Infocom employee

Flexstyles: The Good and Bad Ways We Manage Relationships Between Work and Personal Life

Whether you know it or not, you already have a strategy for handling your life. But is it a conscious strategy? Do you feel in control of your life? Do you have a meaningful understanding of what is driving your work and life relationships and how this feeds into day-to-day well-being for yourself and those with whom you regularly live and interact?

Or maybe you are like Haley. You know that you experience ongoing tension between your job and personal life, but you're not sure what the root causes of these tensions are. You just know they exist and are always there. You didn't know that there is any other way of living.

Although you probably have access to some work-family or flexibility policies offered by your employer, they don't seem to be helping you make your work and family demands mesh better. They aren't meeting your needs. Sure, you may have a great job—on paper at least. Maybe even a graduate degree and a house with a picket fence (or a cool rent-free apartment with an imaginary one). You have a partner you love living with, a pet, and maybe even a child or two. Or if you are single, you may yearn for this kind of family some day. But why aren't you happy? Why are you always feeling stressed and overloaded? Why isn't your life the way you dreamed it would be? Why can't you stop thinking about work when you are supposed to be relaxing? And why are you always bombarded with non-work stuff to handle when you actually want to be focusing on your job? Why do you feel like you lack control over your life?

The answer, for many of us, is perhaps you haven't understood that you have developed a flexstyle. If you are like most people, your current approach just evolved over time through a series of ad hoc (and sometimes not optimal) choices. Would you like to know whether there is a better way?

In this chapter, we reveal two main ideas to help you begin to take control to be the CEO of your life. The first idea is that we all have a flexstyle—the psychological and physical ways we manage relationships between our job and personal life. We will share with you what a flexstyle is, why it is important, and some examples of how people get into flexstyle routines, through making a number of unconscious or conscious decisions. It is only when people understand their patterns of flexstyle behaviors and how their flexstyle works within the structures of their current work and family environment that they will be able to make changes to be more in control and create healthier work-life relationships.

The second thing to learn is that there are three main types of flexstyles, and under each type is a good and bad way of feeling about how we use flexibility. Under each flexstyle, there is one subgroup where people feel in control and happy with their lives. Under the other subgroup, people are unhappy and feel out of control. So, on the surface, under each flexstyle type, people can look like they are managing work and life relationships the same way. But why is it that one individual is totally miserable and the other is at peace? Why is it that what works well for one person can be horrible for the other?

The answer to this question is that what matters most is

- Whether you feel in control of these relationships
- The degree that you perceive alignment between your flexstyle and values for how you would prefer to allocate the life buckets described in Chapter One, "Are You the CEO of Your Working Life?"

When you perceive a fit between your values and your flexstyle, your work and personal life can even enrich or complement each other. At a minimum, they are a neutral influence on the other. But when you don't perceive a fit, your work and personal life usually compete and are at odds. They deplete resources from each other because you are expending extra energy constantly managing conflicting pressures. So when your flexstyle isn't working for you, it isn't fitting with your preferences and identity for how you want to allocate your time and energy across your many life interests. Then your stress increases and your personal effectiveness plummets, whether at the office, at home, or within your community. You often feel tired by managing competing tensions and needing to expend extraordinary resources just to hold things together. If you feel you are beginning to lack control over parts of your life that matter to you, identifying your style will be an important first step before attempting some of the change tactics suggested in the last half of this book. It is also important to note that you can change your flexstyle as you go through your life, as your priorities, job, and personal life circumstances change. You can also change your definition of what is a "workable life"—a life that is working for you. So you may align or realign how you enact your flexstyle as your life buckets shift and evolve as you go through personal changes over your life span—as you leave school, get a job, develop your career, find a new partner, have kids, or move to a new city. Your flexstyle also could change at different times of the year, particularly if you have major shifts in job or family demands that are seasonal. An example might be a ski instructor who works a different job in the off season or a noncustodial parent who has a child live with them during the summer. But for any typical week of our life, most of us have a dominant flexstyle that best describes our approach for managing personal and work relationships.

Types of Flexstyles

There are three main flexstyles that individuals use to build their working lives: *Integrators, Separators, and Volleyers.* In a nutshell, Integrators blend work and personal life physically in terms of time, schedules, and space or location. Psychologically, they also mix work and personal life in terms of their day-to-day thoughts, emotions, and energy. They have difficulty drawing lines between work and family.

Separators segment work from personal life psychologically and physically. For example, they focus on work when at work and on home when at home. They tend not to work at home or on the weekends, but if they have to do so, they are good at creating a separate space for working at home (maybe a home office with a door). Or they can carve out a separate block of time to go in and work and get things done. *Volleyers* switch back and forth, at times experiencing work and life as tightly demarcated from each other and at other times mixing all aspects of their life. For each of these styles of how people manage work and personal life, there are subgroups in which one group is happy and in control, and the other group is feeling unhappy, not in control, and their values are compromised. (See Table 2.1.)[1]

Table 2.1 *Flexstyles*

Well-Being/ Happiness Level	Integrators	Volleyers	Separators
High	Fusion Lover	Quality Timer	Firsters
(Feeling in control; work and personal life have positive relationships.)			(Work or Family First)
Low (Overwhelmed, overworked, out of control; work and personal life often feel at odds.)	Reactors	Job Warriors	Captives

Flexstyle Category 1: Integrators

Integrators continually blend work and nonwork activities during the day. They can be found in a wide range of roles and work settings, including office and factory roles, managerial or professional jobs, and work performed from home. Under this category, we identified two subgroups. The first is *Fusion Lovers*, who experience blending as positive, feeling in control, and fitting with their life values. The second is *Reactors*, who dislike the fact they are blending and feel out of control and unhappy with how they are living their lives because it doesn't fit with their personal preferences. They would rather keep work and personal life separate. They are unhappy and feeling out of control because they aren't managing their lives the way they want.

Fusion Lovers

> *I hop back and forth all the time. When I hear "boundaries," I hear "restrictive and inflexible." I don't view my arrangement and the way I have my company and work set up as restrictive and inflexible. Yes, there are many times I have been cooking dinner and I take a work call. I don't view it as a hassle, I see it as a benefit of flexibility. I want to have it all. I want to run this company and keep it going and be part of my kids' lives, be the great wife to my husband. The motivation around that chaos is I am able to touch all these different areas by having the flexibility to work until midnight. I am able to go out to lunch with a friend in the neighborhood and then work as late into the evening as I need to.*
>
> *Alyssa, business consultant*

Fusion Lovers like Alyssa enjoy switching between work and nonwork responsibilities during the day. They choose to make themselves available to take personal phone calls at the office or to respond to the needs of their spouse or children when required. Many of them also feel comfortable allowing work to bleed into their evenings and weekends. They typically relish extensive participation in many different work and nonwork roles at any one time. Indeed, they thrive on remaining connected to their professional, family, community, and personal responsibilities simultaneously. Perhaps you know them: They're the ones who email their spouse during a meeting to see whether their teenaged daughter passed her driver's license test. Or they brainstorm solutions to a complex business problem while on the way to visit an elderly parent. Or they phone their neighbor during the morning commute to go over plans for the community fundraiser that they're organizing for the upcoming weekend.

Fusion Lovers view multitasking as an efficient and desirable way to live. To them, this flexstyle helps them save valuable time and enables them to fulfill their responsibilities across numerous dimensions of their lives. For instance, Joshua, a project manager who telecommutes several days a week, takes a mini-break in his home office when he's bored or tired or when he runs into a snag with his work. During his breaks, he throws a load of laundry into the washing machine, calls the plumber to make an appointment to hook up the new faucet in the bathroom, or works out a training program to prepare for an upcoming road race. Similarly, Mary, a plant manager at a large manufacturing company, takes a short break after spending a few hours on a report and uses the time to write a thank-you note to friends who recently hosted her for dinner. Meanwhile, Seth, an accountant, decides to check his work e-mail on a Saturday after finishing up yard chores, so he can deal with any urgent issues right away rather than being burdened by them on Monday morning when he's back in the office.

In each of the preceding examples, the Fusion Lover switches from role to role in response to his or her own internal cues—the need to "clear my head" between projects, the desire to "recharge my batteries" by introducing some variety, the wish to gain the satisfaction that comes from "cooking on all four burners," or the effort to keep unsavory tasks (such as responding to e-mails) from stacking up all at once.

Fusion Lovers may also willingly and happily switch roles in response to external cues. To illustrate, a colleague phones Mary during the evening to discuss a work problem, and Mary promptly stops helping her child with homework so that she can take the call. Or Seth leaves his cell phone on during a business meeting so he won't miss the call he's expecting from his physician about some test results. Although this way of working is great if your values are such that you prefer to constantly mix work and personal life, for others such as reactors, integrating work and non-work creates difficulties because the individual is not in control.

Reactors

I basically have to work all the time—long hours, weekends, and I'm available by cell phone 24/7. When I'm at home, I try not to think about work, but that's tough because I feel responsible for my parts in production, and if something goes wrong and causes downtime, I end up having to deal with some personal things during work time, even though I'd rather keep them separate. When you are at the office six to seven days a week and are there [at the office] twelve hours a day, it is impossible not to integrate your roles.

Paul, materials coordinator

Like Fusion Lovers, Reactors shift frequently between work and nonwork activities, often handling family or personal issues while at work and dealing with professional issues while at home. And Reactors work in a wide range of settings—small companies, large firms, telecommuting offices, and home businesses. Yet, unlike Fusion Lovers, Reactors feel they have little control over whether to integrate or compartmentalize the work and nonwork dimensions of their lives. They respond to whatever work or nonwork tasks they believe most need their attention at the time. Many of them feel that they're always "on call" to handle family or personal needs while they're at work and that work pressures inexorably "bleed" into their home lives during their time off. Numerous Reactors would prefer to have greater control over when, where, and how they blend their many responsibilities.

Reactors mix work and nonwork life for several reasons. Some have little or no support in grappling with professional and personal demands. For instance, Ruth, a single parent, has no choice but to leave the office and pick up her son from daycare early when he gets sick: No one else is around to help pitch in. Or Monty, a manager at a large corporation, has to handle a midday phone call from a banker regarding his mortgage application because Monty's spouse is unwilling to deal with such tasks. Many Reactors also shoulder both heavy workloads and family or personal demands. Feeling that they have too much on their plate while at work *and* at home, they conclude that they have no choice but to multitask.

Some Reactors give greater weight to nonwork demands in their integration strategy. Consider Marcus, an information technology professional who works from home for a company and is the father of several young children. After his wife was transferred to a job that required her to work at a corporate office, Marcus began taking on more child-care responsibilities at home during his workday. He puts in 14 to 18 hours per week taking care of the children before and after their school day and is frequently interrupted by the kids during his workday while he's trying to write code. At times, he programs while his two-year-old son sits in his lap. He feels isolated and trapped in a situation that he would not have wanted had he felt he had more control over his choice.

Other Reactors emphasize work priorities, often because they strongly identify themselves through their professional life. Many of these individuals let work seep into personal time during evenings, weekends, and holidays. They may fear that if they didn't "download the office" in this way, they would fail to keep up with the job and possibly get fired. Consider Jane, a senior finance executive, who is married with two teenagers. She sets her own hours, which tend to be long, and works from both her home and office. She feels she has too much work to do in too little time and wishes she didn't have to work at night. As she explains, "My office is two hours from my home [by train], so I work a good hour and a half each way [while commuting], and I count that as part of my workday. I generally spend ten hours in the office and then approximately three hours on the train, and then I'll come home and work for another hour. I will do ten-to-twelve-hour days at home when I work there."

Still other Reactors respond equally promptly to both work and nonwork demands. Cynthia, for example, is an independent consultant who left a demanding corporate job to help start a small consulting firm. Her husband is earning his MBA at night and holding down a difficult corporate job during the daytime. Owing to her spouse's schedule, Cynthia handles all the child-care and family responsibilities in her household as well as meeting the demands of her new professional role.

How Integrators Implement Their Flexstyle

As the preceding vignettes reveal, Integrators blend work and family through a wide variety of means. For example, one single parent who has to leave work early to pick up a child from daycare with a stomachache may depart the office immediately and try to work from home later in the day. Another might pick up the child and, if he's okay, ask a neighbor to watch the youngster and then return to work.

Yet all Integrators share some similarities in how they manage work and non-work commitments. They *physically integrate* by mixing their use of spaces—for instance, drafting a report on their laptop at the kitchen table while the kids are watching TV or taking a moment during the workday to balance a checking account at their desk. They *mix work and nonwork mentally and emotionally*, such as mulling over a business-related problem while participating in a book discussion group or worrying about a spouse's job interview while taking part in a business meeting. For instance, Charles uses his morning break at the office to take calls from his elderly mother to hear how she's doing at the nursing home. And Susan uses business conference calls to take the opportunity to read incoming emails from her spouse.

Having examined integrator styles, let's turn now to separators, a completely different flexstyle.

Flexstyle Category 2: Separators

Separators keep work and nonwork activities compartmentalized throughout the day. Some make their professional life their top priority, and some make their personal or family life their top priority, and they take steps to prevent any blending of the two. Other Separators feel that, owing to the structure of their jobs or the demands of their nonwork life, they have little or no choice but to keep work and non-work in different "buckets."

As with Integrators, we've identified two strategies that make up the Separators category: Firsters (Work or Family) and Captives. These flexstyles are distinguished by how much control people feel they have in using their current approach and how satisfied they are with their situation. Captives do not feel in control of the fact that one part of their life—either their job or their family demands—forces them to overly focus on one part of life to the sacrifice of the other.

In contrast, firsters feel in control of the fact their flexstyle involves separation between work and personal life. They choose to place one part of their life—either work or family—in the highest priority. For Work Firsters, it is time to focus on their jobs that comes first in life. For Family Firsters, it is family or personal life that matters most.

Firsters (Work or Family)

I am a worker for the company during business hours. So they have all my attention and skills. And I'm an achiever. I like to achieve at everything. If I am working at home, it's only on evenings or weekends, and even then my husband knows not to interrupt. My attitude toward work is when you're at work, you work. I look at myself as more than the average person who's at work just to get a paycheck. I am at work because I want to be a professional woman. I want to grow within the company.

Anna, financial consultant for Datatel

Firsters (work or family) identify themselves primarily through their professional lives *or* their nonwork lives. What matters most to firsters is that one part of their life is paramount. (By "Family," we also mean personal, community, spiritual, and other priorities that don't fall within the realm of work.) Work or Family Firsters feel they have extensive control over how they arrange their lives, and they're generally satisfied with their current situation.

Bob, for instance, is a Work Firster who makes his professional responsibilities his top priority. He loves his job as a senior business consultant and accepts that succeeding in this career requires him to be available at all hours to clients and global customers. He often works late into the night. "I work more at home," he says. "Because I'm here in the evening, I'll log in and send some e-mails. Or when the workday is over, I'll keep working, and the next thing I know, it'll be seven or eight at night. But I'll be on a roll, even if other people at the office are leaving. I also work more on weekends, because my computer's here, and I can log on and do a few things. I definitely think I work more hours. But the bottom line is I really enjoy the freedom and the comfort, and I don't mind the hours."

Family Firsters consider their family or personal life more important than their careers. Take Bethany, who works in human resources and is married with three children. She is adamant about keeping her family and work life separate, specifically so she can give her children her full attention when she's home. When she's at work, she focuses on her job responsibilities. For instance, if one of her children needs to come home early from school because he's sick, Bethany arranges for a friend or neighbor to pick him up and stay with him until she gets home. But when Bethany is home, her attention is entirely on her family, with the goal of making her children feel special.

It is important to note that Family Firsters don't necessarily need to have a spouse or children. They could be a family of one. Whether one is a Family

Firster is not based on one's family background, but whether an individual's dominant values are to design life decisions to enable a focus on personal time—whether it is for themselves or personal interest or for being with family. Family Firsters' needs to have a "life" are a high personal priority. Many spoke of highly valuing either "Time for Me or Personal Interests," or "Time for My Family."

So not all Firsters select spending time with family as an alternative priority to work. Consider Nate, who shares an apartment with several housemates and is actively involved in community outreach and neighborhood volunteer efforts. Nate works as a quality control expert for a manufacturing company. Though he enjoys his job, he works a strict eight-hour day so that he can focus sharply on his external interests during his time off.

Captives

I work in a manufacturing plant, ensuring production quality, and we've achieved some of the highest quality in the world. We are very lean. But this means that my usual days are 6:00 a.m. to 5:00 p.m. or 6:00 p.m, and I often even end up staying after that for the next shift. Last Christmas we had plant closure for a week, but I needed to make sure that suppliers were doing what they were meant to, and so I came into work. There isn't much of my job that I could do at home, so I'm in the plant all the time, which makes it hard to take care of personal needs sometimes. My wife and I are expecting, and she's had a difficult pregnancy and wants me to come to all her doctor visits, but it's just so hard for me to get away very often. I want to support her and ensure the baby's okay, but I just don't have a lot of flexibility.

Max, production manager

Some Separators segment the work and nonwork aspects of their lives because their jobs or other dimensions of their lives don't lend themselves to any other approach. Perhaps they work for a company that doesn't allow flextime or telecommuting, or their job, by its very nature, must be done only in the office. Or maybe their company's culture is such that people get ahead only by putting in extensive "face time" at the office. For a Separator who prioritizes family life, perhaps the lack of a partner at home means that the person must keep work from bleeding into evenings and weekends so he can care for children. We refer to such individuals as Captives, reflecting their sense of being trapped in either their career role or their nonwork role.

Nadia's situation exemplifies the Captives strategy. She has a human resources job in a company that forbids her to take work home because of the confidential nature of the information she handles. Her boss also prefers to supervise her by seeing her face-to-face and by meeting frequently with her. The company is structured such that Nadia is the only person in the firm who is familiar with the Human Resources (HR) department's many responsibilities; no one else at the company can serve as a backup if she's not in the office. Moreover, she's an HR generalist; thus, she helps her many internal "customers" with a wide range of HR-related issues—everything from payroll problems, health-insurance claims processing, 401(k) decisions, and so forth. To do her job, she must have well-publicized hours during which employees and managers can count on having access to her. For these reasons, Nadia cannot bring work home even if it has piled up to a worrisome extent—and even if she would like to work from home at times.

How Separators Implement Their Flexstyle

Separators—whether they put work or non-work first, or whether they feel captured in the professional or nonprofessional dimension of their lives—use a wide variety of means in any given day. They compartmentalize work and other dimensions of their lives. It doesn't matter whether they work in a traditional office or manufacturing plant setting or in flexible work arrangements that include working part- or full-time from home. What matters is how they psychologically perceive their lives as organized into fairly discrete buckets.

Separators use physical space, time, and mental perceptions to manage their responsibilities—in this case, to keep work and non-work in different compartments. For example, Rosa, who puts her family first despite enjoying her job as a training manager, avoids taking extra work home (physical separation). She addresses personal tasks early in the morning or during the evening, so she can concentrate on work while she's in the office (temporal separation). If she wants to spend more focused time with her family, she uses paid vacation days (temporal separation). She also feels fine about hiring a trusted daycare provider to look after her children during the workday so that she doesn't have to worry about her children when she is not watching them (mental separation). And she has actively sought to report to a manager who trusts her, values her on-the-job contributions, and respects her focus on family (mental separation).

Carl also puts family first, though he is self-employed and has a home office. He prevents work from leaking into his family responsibilities by working from an office that is separate from the rest of his house. The office has its own door and a separate phone and data line. In addition, Carl has two different email accounts—work and personal. During the workday, family members aren't allowed to enter Carl's office. And at five o'clock each day, he leaves the office and locks the door. He refuses to sneak back in to check e-mail after his workday ends and the kids have gone to bed. Like Rosa, Carl relies on daycare providers to look after his children during the workday.

Flexstyle Category 3: Volleyers

Some men and women—we've dubbed them Volleyers—integrate the work and nonwork aspects of their lives at times and separate them at other times, depending on their priorities and the circumstances of their professional and home or personal life. We've identified two flexstyles that make up this category: Quality Timers and Job Warriors. Again, these flexstyles are distinguished by the degree of control people feel they have over how they're managing their lives, as well as their level of satisfaction with the current quality of their lives.

Quality Timers

I work in a satellite office, where I focus just on work for most of the day but have recently started to telework for part of the day so I can deal with some personal needs. My mother is the primary caregiver for my grandmother who's in her 90s and also for my father who is in his 70s and has heart problems. I'm the only family member in town who can help and so I take my lunch hour at my parents' home so I can help out. I'm happy to give my mother a break and to get this time with my father.

Rick, web-based project manager

Quality Timers use time cues—such as the shift from the workweek to the weekend or from a busy time of year to a not-so-busy time—to decide when to integrate or separate work and nonwork dimensions of their lives. Generally satisfied with their lives, they feel that they have a significant degree of control over their situation.

For example, Susan, an accountant with children in elementary school, works intensely during the tax season—putting in as many as 60 hours a week during February, March, and April. Work comes first during this busy time of year, and family comes second. During tax season, she relies on her husband to take charge of the family's daily scheduling and activities, including ferrying the kids to and from school. Yet in the summer months, Susan reduces her workload considerably and spends far more time with her youngsters when they're on summer vacation. She readily interrupts work to focus on her family when needed during these months.

Though Susan concentrates entirely on work during her busy season, overall she gives her job and her family equal priority. Susan's story also highlights the sense of control and satisfaction many Quality Timers feel regarding their situation. For instance, Susan has a supportive spouse who can shoulder family responsibilities during her busy time of the year that enables her to perceive choice—to manage work and nonwork life to enable quality time at both. If she had no such support, she might well feel that she had significantly less control. She also has elected to work in a profession that, by its very nature, presents a lighter workload during the summer season, when she enjoys concentrating more on her family.

Other Quality Timers use different time cues to decide when to volley between separating and integrating. Consider Janice, a book editor for a publishing company and mother of two young children. Janice's partner, Sylvia, works part-time. On Monday through Wednesday, the days during which Sylvia works, Janice works at the office—focusing entirely on her job while the children are in daycare. Thus, during these days, Janice separates work and nonwork life. But on Thursdays and Fridays, the days when Sylvia isn't working, Janice telecommutes. She does this to spend some time with Sylvia and the kids, even as she handles some work projects during those days. She integrates work and non-work on those two days of the week.

Lauren is another example of a Quality Timer. Married with no children, Lauren works as a freelance writer. She has a small hobby farm that is home to goats and chickens, as well as numerous house pets. Her husband works for an engineering company. Lauren's business is boom and bust—sometimes she has a heavy workload, and sometimes the load eases up. During busy times, she integrates work and non-work, allowing her job to bleed into nights, weekends, holidays, and even vacations if necessary to meet deadlines. Her husband cares for the animals during such high-tempo times. Lauren has just one phone line for home and business, as well as one e-mail account for personal and work—additional signs of integration. Yet she strives to compartmentalize work and non-work when business is booming, by relying on caller identification to avoid taking personal phone calls and by ignoring personal e-mails. When the workload eases, Lauren becomes a Fusion Lover—mixing professional and personal communications throughout the day and taking work breaks to dispatch barn and household chores.

Job Warriors

One hundred percent of my work time is spent traveling. I leave home Sunday night to fly to customer sites, and I'm there Monday through Friday. It's not the perfect arrangement but we've come to accept it. It brings in a paycheck. It's hardest on the kids, but we make up for it with quality time on the weekends.

Jeff, senior systems engineer

Job Warriors face more constraints in when and how they switch between integrating and separating work and non-work. Often in jobs that require them to work from the road as well as at the office and from home, Job Warriors frequently compartmentalize professional and personal activities while traveling for work or working from the office. They tend to mix the career and personal or family dimensions of their lives while working from home. Many of them feel that their job structure or family or personal circumstances leave them little or no control over how they manage conflicting demands. These individuals often have jobs with heavy workloads and simply too much to do in too little time. Sure they have some latitude over when and where they do it, but the physical workload or the travel demands give them limited slack at times over when they integrate and when they separate. So they go through periods of high integration when they feel they are in control and can blend as they need to—often when travel or workloads are not so high—and then they go through periods of high separation when they are forced to separate. In one week, they could move from being on a global trip or working until midnight on a client proposal during the height of tax season, to going to a day or two of being the only one watching the kids because now it is their partner's turn to focus on work because the partner has been covering for the Job Warrior.

Take Raul, a consultant and project startup expert for a global company. Raul's 3,000 coworkers are located in Central and South America as well as the U.S. East Coast, where he lives. Three weeks out of every month, he travels extensively to Latin America by air, consulting on new projects such as the establishment of communications networks between the North and South American continents. During these weeks, he often has late-night dinners with clients. While on the road, he strives to build a sense of team identity with his colleagues, especially in the initial phases of a project. In the fourth week of each month, he telecommutes from a home office. Though he can set his own hours, he typically puts in 60 or more hours per week.

Raul doesn't mind telecommuting from home, including participating in strategy discussions with colleagues over the phone. And he relishes the weeks during which he doesn't have to travel. On telecommuting days, he separates work and non-work by stopping work at four o'clock in the afternoon and spending time in the late afternoon and evening with his wife and two school-age children. On traveling days, he integrates by responding to family phone calls and personal e-mails as needed. Though he enjoys his job, Raul wishes he had more control over when and how often he must be on the road. He and his wife have discussed the stresses of the job and have begun acknowledging the burden his schedule puts on their family life. His wife feels stuck in her career, because she always has to be the one to restructure her job to cover for her husband because he has to travel so much.

How Volleyers Implement Their Flexstyle

Like Integrators, Volleyers use physical, temporal, and mental tactics to implement their flexstyles. For example, Quality Timer Marian, an information technology consultant, works two days a week onsite at a major client company and three days a week from home. While working from home, she makes her children breakfast before school and has a snack with them after school, dealing with job responsibilities during the middle of the day. She also lets her family know that it's okay to interrupt her—but only for specific, agreed-upon reasons—during her workday, and she stops working to let the dog out when he signals the need. So she sends cues to others on when she is available for integrating, and she also structures her day in this way. Then for part of the week she uses physical barriers to separate. It works well for her and is a good style because she controls when she is integrating and separating.

What's Your Flexstyle? Where Do You Fit In?

So now you understand flexstyles—what they are, when they are likely to make you feel like you have positive relationships between work and personal life, and when they are likely to make you feel like relationships between work and personal life are at odds. After reading the preceding descriptions of flexstyles, you may already know whether you're an Integrator, Volleyer, or Separator. But it may be more difficult to determine which strategy you use within that category. If you're an Integrator, are you a Fusion Lover or a Reactor? If you're a Separator, are you a Work or Family Firster or a Captive? If a Volleyer, are you a Quality

Timer or Job Warrior? Clues to your strategy include how much control you believe you have in managing your life demands, as well as how satisfied you are with the current quality of your life. For readers who need help clarifying their overall flexstyle, we provide the following self-assessments. If you feel the need, take several moments to complete this instrument.

Self-Assessment: Identifying Your Flexstyle
Part One: Discerning Your Overall Flexstyle Category

This part of the self-assessment helps you determine whether you're an Integrator, Separator, or Volleyer. Read each statement. Circle the number indicating how much you agree or disagree with the statement. Then follow the instructions for calculating and interpreting your results.

Statement	Strongly Agree	Agree	Neither Agree nor Disagree	Disagree	Strongly Disagree
1. All in all, I try to keep work and personal life separated most of the time.	1	2	3	4	5
2. Except in an emergency, I generally try to take care of personal or family needs at work only when I'm on break or during my lunch hour.	1	2	3	4	5
3. During my workday, there is very little blurring of boundaries between time spent on work and time spent on personal activities.	1	2	3	4	5
4. It is clear where my work life ends and my family or personal life begins.	1	2	2	4	5
5. I rarely attend to personal or family issues during the workday.	1	2	3	4	5
6. I almost never do extra work after normal work hours.	1	2	3	4	5
7. In general, I don't take work-related phone calls or e-mails during evenings, weekends, holidays, or vacations.	1	2	3	4	5

Statement	Strongly Agree	Agree	Neither Agree nor Disagree	Disagree	Strongly Disagree
8. In general, I talk as little as possible about my family or personal issues with most people I work with.	1	2	3	4	5
9. I usually handle e-mails related to my family or personal life separately from e-mails related to my work.	1	2	3	4	5
10. When I'm at home, I rarely think about work, so I can fully get away from my job.	1	2	3	4	5
11. If I work or ever were to work from home, I would work in a space that is designated for that purpose only.	1	2	3	4	5
12. I do not think about my family, friends, and personal interests when at work, so I can focus.	1	2	3	4	5
13. With most of my family and friends, I tend not to talk about work issues as I like to keep work separate.	1	2	3	4	5
14. If I work from home (or were ever to work from home) I make it clear that family and friends should not interrupt me unless it is important to do so.	1	2	3	4	5
15. If I work from home (or were ever to work from home) I wouldn't handle household or family responsibilities until the workday is finished.	1	2	3	4	5
Calculating your score: Add up the total number of circles you placed in each column, and write the totals in the boxes to the right.					

Interpreting your score: If you circled "1" and "2" for most of the statements, you are likely a Separator. If you circled "4" or "5" for most of the statements, you are probably an Integrator. If you circled a wide variety of statements, ranging between 1 and 5, you are probably a Volleyer.

Closing

Now you are probably saying, "Okay, great." I now know my flexstyle. But why does it matter what I am? Each of the flexstyles introduced in this chapter has unique pros and cons. If you know your general flexstyle (for example, Integrator, Separator or Volleyer) but still aren't sure whether you are using flexibility in a way that generally makes you feel good and that has a positive impact on you and those you live and work with, see the appendix, "Flexstyle Web Site and Overview Assessments," at the end of this book. These additional assessments can help you take a closer look at how your work and personal life relationships are affecting your well-being and effectiveness on and off the job. You may already think you know how you feel about how you are using flexibility, but these additional assessments can help you clarify whether you are using flexibility positively or negatively. If you are already sure you know who you are—for example, whether you are a Fusion Lover or a Reactor, or a Captive, or Work or Family Firster—you are ready to move on to the next chapter where you will be introduced to the idea of flexstyle tradeoffs to help you begin the journey of thinking about the advantages and disadvantages of your style and whether your style is generally working well for you.

chapter three

Weighing the Tradeoffs

I feel like my career is a marathon and they want me to sprint the entire way. I can't seem to change my flexstyle even though I now have the freedom to do so and my family life situation has changed from when I started out in my career. Because I have always been a top performer, I probably could cut back a little, and no one at work would even notice, but it just isn't working out. I tried to cut back after my second child. I had always been on the high potential list and received numerous "atta-girls" at work and before that at school, but I am still working way too much. Now that I have two kids under six and I am still working full time, I find that I am becoming overloaded on both work and family demands. I am now sacrificing sleep and personal time. I don't understand why I can't make things work better, I have a good track record and a job with flexibility, but I can't seem to work less even though I would much rather spend more time with my kids now.

Recently, I tried to restructure my work arrangements to enable me to work from home one day a week. The good news is I am now able to walk my five year old home from the bus after she gets out of kindergarten, which I love. But the bad news is after she is home from school, and the baby is napping, I can't seem to stop working. Even though I have been up since 5:00 a.m. and already worked an eight-hour day, and my boss is okay with me not being available Friday afternoons unless there is an emergency at work, I feel guilty ending my workday when my daughter gets home because I have so much to do. So after she gets home from school, I am still worrying about my clients, still trying to work, and I don't feel 'mentally there' but am still thinking about my job. This is a bummer since one of the reasons I asked to work from home on Fridays was to have the freedom to be home and have some extra time with my children. I notice it makes my kids stressed to see me constantly running back and forth to e-mails and phone calls all Friday afternoon.

Erin's Story: Addicted to Work First

Erin is one of those habitual Work Firsters—people who learned over their lives that what worked best in managing relationships between work and personal life was to put work first. Now that she has two kids and is established in her career, she would like to change her style to become more of a Quality Timer. *Yet no matter how hard she tries, she finds she can't.* Her prevailing company culture and own self-induced pressure to continue to overachieve are getting in the way. She is finding that she is unable to truly change her old flexstyle that had worked so well for her and paid off for so many years. She is having difficulty unlearning habits that used to work so well for her, even though her career stage and family stage have changed. Maybe you see some of the tradeoffs of your own style in Erin's story of how she is managing flexibility between work and personal life. Or you, your spouse, or someone you work with may be reflected in one of the other stories we share in the coming chapters.

All flexstyles, even those that make us feel happy and in control in the short run, can be hard to change. This is particularly the case for people who are juggling demanding careers and are aware that they must make some difficult tradeoffs. Erin thought that her decision to work from home one day a week would be an effective strategy to help her change her work first style. But because she has a demanding career, too much work to do in too little time, and is unwilling to cut back or ask for help (notice she didn't mention talking to either her husband or boss on how they might help her manage her rising workload on and off the job to live better), she is unable to change. Many of us may see ourselves in Erin. We sometimes can be our own worst enemy in creating our own work-life conflicts. We may not take the time to fully understand how we are trapped and driven to established patterns that constrain us. We keep managing relationships in the same old ways that aren't working so well, something we are unlikely to stop doing unless we start looking at the tradeoffs. These tradeoffs can be small and nuanced but are often critical to understand in order to make an even small and incremental change. Not everything we do in how we manage work and family is totally good or bad as the stereotyped images in the media may have us believe. There are shades of gray that we need to understand to make a change. Otherwise we may be stuck and unable to see the underlying dynamics of how we are currently managing things that keeps us trapped from imagining new possibilities.

Preparing for Change: Understanding the Tradeoffs of Different Flexstyles

To create real change that enables us to take control as CEOs of our lives, we cannot continue to make choices without recognizing the downsides of these choices. We must take off the blinders that keep us from seeing that there are more options and ways of living and managing our flexstyle. The inability to see what is creating some problems can be magnified when we have a major change in our life or work situation as Erin did. We may be unaware that there is a menu of different ways to manage relationships between professional and personal life that we hadn't even seen as possibilities. We just keep adding more and more to our current way of living. Or we may be stuck in old belief systems. We may be out of touch with our changing values, particularly if we have not recently assessed how we ideally would like to allocate our life buckets. Just slowing down and taking the time to clarify what matters most to us and weighing the tradeoffs of different flexstyles is a huge first step to change. We must see how these values are reflected and the degree to which things are working or not working in the ways we would like. Are we truly living the life we would like to be living? Are we allocating our time, energy, psyche, and space in how we are currently managing work and home relationships in ways that are effectively aligned with these core beliefs?

By understanding the tradeoffs associated with each flexstyle, you can more easily decide whether you want to make small or major changes to your style to mitigate its downsides. There are some changes that all people make regardless of their styles to make their lives better, which we discuss in Chapter 7, "Changes Everyone Can Make to Improve Quality of Life." Then there are others changes specific to each style, and in Chapter 8, "Tailoring Change to Your Particular Flexstyle," we examine these change strategies. In Chapter 9, "Negotiating a New Flexstyle and a Life That Works on Your Terms," you learn how to negotiate with others to support change. In Chapter 10, "Not Going It Alone: Making Sustainable Change at Your Workplace," you think about how to manage and sustain flexstyles to change organizations.

Tradeoff Tenets

There are several main tenets to keep in mind regardless of your flexstyle. The *first* is that *every style has tradeoffs*. Unfortunately no style is perfect. You need to recognize these tradeoffs and conduct some self-reflection on what tradeoffs you absolutely could not live with, before attempting to make changes to your flexstyle.

The *second* tenet is the *importance of consciously making a choice on which flexstyle would offer you the best alignment with your values*. You must take action. Otherwise, people in your life such as your boss or your family will make decisions that take away your ability to make choices. Not making a choice is actually making a choice to let others decide your flexstyle.

Third, although there is no perfect style, *some of these flexstyles, such as Reactors, Captives, or Job Warriors, are not sustainable over time or good for our mental and physical health and those of family members we live with*. These generally are styles where we are not feeling in control, those that truly can take away our ability to have personal power over the meshing of work and personal life. When flexstyles of any stripe are forced on us—when we consciously or unconsciously live our lives in ways different than our preferences and identities suggest, we feel like we have little control over our lives. Stress increases, and well-being takes a nosedive in how we experience our personal mastery of interactions at the office, at home, or within our communities. If you feel you are beginning to lack control over parts of your life that matter to you, then identifying your style and understanding its tradeoffs will be an important first step to try before attempting some of the change tactics suggested in the last half of this book.

In general, having more control and the ability to chose when you separate between work and family and when you integrate is good and will make your life better. The exception to this rule is when you are in an excessive workload situation—you have simply too much to do at work and at home. In this case, changing how you manage your flexstyle will be insufficient to help you successfully make sustainable life changes.

This leads to the *fourth* rule: *When you have a life that is overloaded with too many work and family demands to realistically regularly handle, minor tinkering with your current flexstyle may not be enough*. You may need to move toward a major style shift. Typically for people with far too much on their plate, the ultimate solution is to make the tough choice to cut back on your total life workload to customize your life to focus on the life buckets that are the most meaningful. You may also consider looking at part-time work or reduced load work options to cut back on work. Minor tactics like not checking email at certain times won't fully help if things keep piling up. Simply using flextime will not help you as you are just shifting the work in time without making it go away on a daily basis. Similarly, trying to telecommute when you are overloaded with too much work at the same time you may be keeping heavy family demands in check just shifts the workload pressures into your family system. You bring your overload and stress into your home. So you may need to think about major flexstyle change.

The *fifth* rule is to *be aware of the fact that when you are undergoing a major personal or professional change, you should be open to reviewing your flexstyle, because it is likely to be out of alignment.* There are key times in over the course of our lives (births, changing or losing jobs, marriage, divorce, death of a loved one, and so on) that may be good times for us to reassess and make some change as we are more receptive and open to change at these key life switching points. We need to make sure we are not driven by career paths as much as our life paths—how we see our journey over the life course that includes both a career and personal self.

In the next chapters, we share with you how first Integrators, then Separators, and then Volleyers weigh the tradeoffs of their styles. You read stories of people we interviewed that illuminate the most defining tradeoffs associated with the different strategies. These tradeoffs can be largely clustered into two main groups: personal and family-related or career and work-oriented.

We need to make sure we are not driven by career paths as much as our life paths.

Besides yourself, you also see your boss, coworkers, friends and family members in the other styles, as most of us work and associate with people who have a wide range of flexstyles. Part of making our own flexstyle work is understanding how well flexstyles work for others. In the chapter that is closest to your style, you can take the self-assessment at the end. These assessments are designed to help you determine whether you would benefit from a change in your flexstyle. They help you determine what's working and what's not working so well for you and enable you to begin the journey of change.

Creating a Life That Works

How do you use flexibility to create a life that works? The approach is deeply personal and cannot succeed unless it fits with two main criteria:

1. **Life bucket preferences.** First, your flexstyle must fit with your preferences for when, where, and how you want to carry out your many life roles and responsibilities. It must reflect your dream for your life buckets you analyzed in Chapter One, "Are You the CEO of Your Working Life?"—the ideal way you want to allocate yourself in your time, energy, and physical access to your family, friends, job, community, and personal needs such as exercise, relaxation, and spirituality.

2. **Personal Identity.** Second, your approach fits with your true vision of yourself—your identity in societal roles that are highly meaningful to you. Basically, it must fit with how you see yourself. That is, how you define your primary purpose(s) in life. Where you find meaningful social relationships with others in your life and your passion in living—for example, successful professional, husband, mother, son—the roles unique to each of us. If we are using a flexstyle that has tradeoffs that keep us from living in a way that jibes with who we are—for example, we feel like we aren't able to be a father in a high-quality way, and this role is highly meaningful to us—we will face deep distress. We need to make change to reduce this tension and mismatch between how we see ourselves and how we are meshing the personal and professional self.

chapter four

Tradeoffs of Using Flexibility for Higher Work-Life Integration

We are in a client-driven business. We have to be available when the clients are available. Even when the kids are home after school, when I hear the phone ring, I know I have to run and take a phone call. It is much more imposing on personal life and children. When I worked in an office setting all day, there were times I missed [work-related] calls when I wasn't at my desk. Now as a partner in my own firm, often working from my home, I feel I have to be available to work all the time.

Cynthia, age 30, mother with two children, managerial consultant

Cynthia: Profile of a Reluctant Reactor

Individuals who integrate use flexibility to blend work and personal life. This can be done both physically, in terms of time, schedules, and space, as well as psychologically, in terms of daily energy, emotions, and thoughts. Yet integrator flexstyles can be a double-edged sword depending on your circumstances and priorities. As Cynthia's comments reveal, even individuals who negotiate new flexibility options, like telecommuting, can still face difficulties in managing work and personal life relationships.

Three years ago, Cynthia worked at Technology, Inc. (a pseudonym), the prestigious global corporation she had joined after getting her master's degree in business from a top program. Technology, Inc., was one of the most admired employers in America and renowned for developing and producing great managers and business leaders. After joining the company, Cynthia steadily received promotions and repeatedly heard that she was on the "high potential list." Her husband was also fortunate to be hired by the same firm. As dual-career up-and-comers, they received promotions to the same new geographic locations every couple of years.

After working at Technology, Inc., for eight years, Cynthia gave birth to two children. Owing to her long tenure there, she was able to take a paid six-week maternity leave after each birth. And when she returned to work after each leave, she put the children into full-time care with a nanny. Cynthia's colleagues often told her that she seemed to have more energy than most people. During these years, she was a quintessential Quality Timer, a Volleyer, who was able to switch her flexstyle easily between Integrating and Separating as needed to fulfill her professional and family responsibilities with equal dedication. Having a physical office away from home in part helped her do this.

Whenever necessary, she easily integrated work and family responsibilities. For example, she neither minded getting up at 5:00 a.m. to get a jump on the workday from home nor would she hesitate to stay up late at night to catch up on e-mail after putting the kids to bed. She developed detailed child-care and pre-school schedules. And she often used her 10-mile commute to run household errands. She was the one who took the kids to the doctor when needed and attended their school events. After handling such responsibilities, she would either return to the office or log in to work from home at night after the children had gone to bed. Sometimes, she was able to bring her children to a playgroup that met late Friday afternoons. She learned how to make easy, quick meals and hired a cleaning professional to come to the house once a week. She even lowered her personal standards about cleanliness and clutter in her home.

At other times, Cynthia separated work and family with little difficulty. For instance, during hours when she was at the office (7:00 a.m. to 6:00 p.m.), she focused entirely on her job responsibilities. Thanks to the arrangements she had made for her family, as well as her impressive powers of organization, she felt secure in the knowledge that her child-care providers had everything under control at home. On the surface, at least, she seemed to be living the life of her dreams.

All this changed when Cynthia and her husband had their second major fight over whose business trip would get priority. Soon after this incident, she decided to leave Technology, Inc., to found a small management consulting firm with a friend. Her rationale for the change? Managing a consultancy, she believed, would enable her to achieve greater flexibility in when, where, and how she worked. For example, if she and her husband experienced a conflict between two business trips, she could change her schedule to work around his. Little did she realize that by quitting and giving up a formal office, she created new problems.

In becoming self-employed, Cynthia did not see herself as "opting out" of the corporate world. She and her business partner leveraged the sterling reputations and plentiful contacts they had built during their corporate careers to launch their nascent business. In her new role, Cynthia performs much of the same work she had in her old job at Technology, Inc., but she now has more of the flexibility she felt she needed. Yet her new arrangement has also presented fresh challenges, as the quotation that opens this section suggests. In particular, she feels pressured to always make herself available to her clients. She also is the one who now does 100% of the child and house stuff, because she has "so much more flexibility." Before, when both she and her husband worked in office corporate settings, they shared household and child care more equally or hired someone to help them and felt okay about it. Now with the lower income, Cynthia doesn't feel comfortable paying a regular sitter.

As a self-employed consultant, Cynthia now uses mainly a Reactor style of integration to manage work and family demands. Feeling that she has little control over the client-driven nature of her consulting work, she tackles and blends professional and family priorities all day long—whether it's during a weekday, late in the evening, or over a weekend. Recently, she had her third child, further increasing her family responsibilities. Owing to her perception of scant control over the strictures of her new job and her resulting frustration with the quality of her life, she has become a Reactor.

Although she sees herself as equally committed to her work and her family, privately Cynthia admits (with great regret in her voice) that it "killed" her to quit a "great job" where she had developed a strong sense of self and a much-admired professional identity. But the long hours, constant travel, and the feeling she was not excelling in either dimension of her life had worn her down. In her words:

When I had my sons, I felt in no way could I compete [in the corporate world]. The long hours I had put in starting out my professional career set a precedent of "This is how Cynthia works." I felt this, even if others didn't make me feel this way. I was a top performer. I could become a "misperformer" or middle performer now with all I had to do at work and home. This was a difficult thing to accept. I was not going to be a top performer like my peers with the new amount of hours I could realistically put in and still be involved with my children the way I wanted to. The reality is people at my former employer stayed late and came in early, and now with technology they can go home and work. And with a family, I couldn't do that. I couldn't work late and put in the long hours at home working every night.

I was never told I was a middle performer. I got out before it could happen. I wanted to be a present mom. But I lost more than half my identity when I left Technology, Inc., and was home with my kids full time for a year. It was such a blow to my ego. I just realized how important work was to me, to realize that I am contributing to helping people. Intrinsically, I love the work

I do. But I also love that I can meet my kids' teachers and take [the children] to school. I love that I have the flexibility to go on a field trip and then can choose to work at my job at night or on the weekend if I want to. I am proud to say I am still working and learning. I also love that my kids see their mom being able to contribute to businesses and still balance things at home. Yet I [still] wish I had more control over when and how I work. I don't think I do a very good job of managing boundaries between work and home very well.

Cynthia's story reveals a common difficulty that can arise with people who use a Reactor integration strategy to manage the work and nonwork dimensions of their lives. Even though she left the corporate world to run her own business, changing *where* she worked has not eradicated the problems she was experiencing at Technology, Inc.; it just created new ones. As we mentioned, all styles have tradeoffs, and Cynthia is still feeling at risk for burnout. She continues to feel a lack of control over how she handles work and family responsibilities. And she still worries that she's not fulfilling either her career or her family priorities as well as she'd like. Clearly, Cynthia continues to let her beliefs about her professional and personal priorities control her—rather than the other way around. And as long as this is true, she will go on feeling dissatisfied with the quality of her life overall.

The lesson? Merely changing your work environment may not be enough to enable you to achieve a fulfilling life. In order to be the CEO of Your Life, you must also consider new ways to exercise greater control over how to meet your shifting needs and priorities, and be open to revisiting your assumptions about how you can live a responsible life. With Cynthia's increasing family responsibilities and new pressures to be available to clients, integrating her professional and home life (as she did at times while working for Technology, Inc.) isn't helping her to feel more competent and satisfied in either role.

Many women have experiences similar to Cynthia's. They feel forced to react—an integration style where they are forced to juggle work and nonwork commitments simultaneously—when a second or third child comes along, when a parent comes down with a debilitating illness, or when a spouse's job demands conflict with their own. Clearly, Cynthia carefully thought through what was most important to her and used those insights to craft the most satisfying life possible. Yet her beliefs about what constitutes a "high performer at work" and "a good mom" have caused her to shoulder such heavy workloads at work and at home that she simply cannot meet the standards she has set for herself in either realm.

Her frustration over feeling pressed to give up a satisfying identity as a talented corporate professional to better handle family responsibilities further contributes to her dissatisfaction. But not everyone who heavily integrates work and personal life is unhappy. Read on.

Alyssa's Story of a Fusion Lover

Alyssa has two elementary school-age children. She owns her own business consulting firm and primarily works from a home office. She said, "The guy who is renting my office address to me told me I should think about having my office there all the time. Yet that defeats the purpose of what I do. Right now I am here in the morning when the kids go to school; I might be working, but I can give them a kiss goodbye. They can color at a desk while I am working. They come in and say hello to me, get a drink, and then go outside. We are very interactive even though I am working. If I got office space, that would defeat the proximity and the closeness. I am not sure what I would gain by having an office outside the home. I am one of two women in my neighborhood who works. People come up to me and say "I am so sorry you have to work." They don't know how much I love doing both. I love hopping in an out of work and family all day long.

	Alyssa's Fusion Loving Approach for Integrating Work and Personal Life
Physical Boundary	Works mostly in the home rather than in the office, even though her company has purchased office space outside the home.
	Takes laptop with her on family vacations at Disney World and at the weekend second home.
	Has cell phone with her while son is at karate class.
Temporal Boundary	Work schedule is different every day and every week.
	Lots of restructuring: Will rearrange work to accommodate fun family and social needs like attending kids' plays or having lunches with neighborhood female friends.
	Works at night and some vacations but does not mind it.
Mental/Emotional and Boundary	Does not want to separate into mental boundaries; sees work family as highly intertwined now. Believes it is difficult to separate work and life. They crisscross all day, not like when she went to a corporate workplace and would disconnect from home.
	Co-mingling and multitasking work and family all day long.

Tradeoffs of Integrating Flexstyles

Cynthia's and Alyssa's stories illuminate some of the tradeoffs that using flexibility to integrate work and personal life can present. Consider these additional challenges posed not only for Reactors but also for even the most satisfied Fusion Lovers:

- **Long days, role creep.** For many Integrators, work demands creep into the nonwork dimensions of their lives—and vice versa, as they handle family or community responsibilities during work hours. During tough economic times especially, people may feel pressured to permit "job creep" because they fear losing employment if they don't do whatever is necessary to fulfill their professional responsibilities.[1] It can feel like you are *always* working, if you get up and work 5:00 a.m. to 7:00 a.m., then get the kids off to school, and return to working from 10:00 a.m. through 3:00 p.m., shift to chauffeuring kids to soccer and gymnastics, and then intersperse spells of family time and work throughout the evening, finally collapsing into bed at midnight. Integrators who allow family to creep into their work lives may also find themselves working longer days to get as much done for the job as someone who separates and devotes herself entirely to work from 8:00 a.m. to 5:00 p.m. every day. For anyone working long workdays, stress and overload may result—and the strategy may not be sustainable in the long run.

- **Others' misunderstanding about availability.** For numerous Integrators, handling some work responsibilities at home can inadvertently send the message to family and friends that it's okay to interrupt. Spouses, children, and even neighbors may drop in to say hello or ask for something on the assumption that the person is available for—and doesn't mind—interruptions. Bosses and coworkers can also misunderstand an Integrator's availability: One supervisor, for example, thought it was perfectly okay to phone her employee at home during early evening hours, over a weekend, and even during a vacation. Or we confuse our kids and family and screw up those social relationships because they see us and think we are available yet we are only there physically. We are mentally absent and in our work persona.

- **Higher switching costs and role restructuring.** To use their flexstyle, many Integrators must be willing to change work- and nonwork-related plans in the eleventh hour. For instance, an unexpected problem arises on an important professional project during a day when Jim was expecting to attend his daughter's recital in the afternoon. So he asks his wife to attend the child's event. Or Ella's dog falls gravely ill while she's working on a time-sensitive report from her home office, and she has to put the work on hold to rush the animal to the vet. Even for the most change-tolerant individuals, constant restructuring and rescheduling of plans can eventually wear thin. The difficulties associated with these kinds of frequent changes are called *switching costs*.[2] Each time people shift focus among the different roles they have (worker, parent, and so on), they must reacquaint themselves with what they were doing before they shifted—all of which eats up time and takes its toll on the brain. This happens across all the different flexstyles but is an issue for Integrators because they shift so often between professional and personal responsibilities during a typical day.

- **Perceptions of professionalism.** In organizational cultures that don't value flexible work arrangements, people who integrate by interrupting their work to deal with personal needs (or handle the barking dog or crying baby out of necessity when the phone rings at the home office) may be perceived by bosses and colleagues as less committed to their work than people who separate. These perceptions can come with a high price tag. A boss may give the Integrator lukewarm performance ratings or withhold or delay a promotion. And peers may decide not to include the person in a highly visible cross functional project team. Or people are simply left out of the water cooler and networking pipeline.

- **Lack of buffers.** Because Integrators are constantly mixing work and family roles, they lack the buffers that Separators and Volleyers have. When something is going badly in one role, the negative dynamics can bleed into the other role. So if you are having a bad day at work and your partner instant messages during the meeting, you are more likely to interact negatively. This is an example of negative spillover when bad things spill over from one role to the other. Although positive spillover can sometimes occur, such as when something good happens in your personal life and you bring that to work, because work is a very powerful force in your life, it is more likely that when bad things happen at work, you will bring more of it into your personal life under an Integrator style.

47

Table 4-1 presents a summary of the tradeoffs we found in our research followed by a discussion of special considerations for reactors.

Table 4-1 *Integrator Flexstyles*

	Pros	Cons
Fusion Lover	Ability to multitask can be efficient for some people in short run. Ability to personally control which is more important to handle at any given time. Feeling of being in touch with both worlds without sacrificing or having to choose which has highest overall precedence. Re-energize by focusing on something different. Helps manage family workload by being able to multitask on breaks.	Job or family creep (long days) Others' escalating expectations about your availability Switching costs from frequent transitions Seen as unprofessional if integrate family or other personal interests into work time Lack of buffers
Reactor	Ability to attend to most immediate need as it occurs.	Job or family creep (long days) Others' escalating expectations about your availability Switching costs from frequent transitions—higher even than other integrators because dislike switching Seen as unprofessional if integrate family into work time Overload and loss of feeling of control Frustration and burnout Dissatisfaction with performance in both work and personal life roles Lack of buffers

Special Considerations for Reactors

Reactors face a slightly different and less desirable set of tradeoffs than Fusion Lovers. Reactors are unhappy with the way that they are balancing their work and personal obligations. They would prefer to find ways to segment demands and to feel like they are more in control of transitions from one realm to the other.

Because they are less comfortable with transitions, and less in control of when and how they occur, Reactors face higher switching or process costs than other Integrators (Fusion Lovers) do. It is more costly to them, in mental energy and emotional exertion, to be pulled from their work to answer a call from a delivery person or to help their children resolve a dispute over a toy or which DVD to watch. More generally, as with all people we studied who found themselves in a particular flexstyle for reasons beyond their control, outcomes are worse. A wide range of research, from studies examining the job satisfaction and performance of people involuntarily in temporary jobs, to studies of the effect of involuntary job role changes on absenteeism, commitment, and other work outcomes, have shown that people do better when they are able to choose.[3]

Self-Assessment Tools on Tradeoffs

If you are an Integrator (Fusion Lover or Reactor), take the self-assessment tools on the tradeoffs presented in this chapter. If you do not have one of these styles, you may want to just go on to the next chapter.

For Integrators: Weighing the Tradeoffs in Your Life

Now that we have introduced the kinds of tradeoffs that many Integrators face, you may want to pause to reflect on whether you also experience these issues, especially if you have learned from Chapter 2, "Knowing Your Flexstyle," that you are an Integrator. To help you do so, we have prepared a number of self-assessment exercises. If you use several styles, you may want to fill out the exercises in this section, as well as those in other portions of later chapters that are targeted at Volleyers and Separators.

The purpose of this exercise is to determine whether the benefits of your current strategy outweigh the costs—or vice versa. When the costs of a flexstyle outweigh the benefits, altering the strategy may be in order. Note, too, that benefits and costs are relevant not only for you but also for others in your work and nonwork lives who are affected by your style. For example, a child left waiting at school for a half-hour because you couldn't leave work on time to pick him up is experiencing a cost related to your style even if it suits you in the immediate run by enabling you to finish up what you were working on for your job. A coworker who can't complete her part of a group project when she wants to because you can never focus on her project long enough because you are constantly switching back and forth between work and personal life is also experiencing a cost. Likewise, a friend with whom you keep canceling dinner plans because you have too much work to do is also experiencing a cost.

Integrator Flexstyle Self-Assessment

For the flexstyle that most resembles the one you use (or primarily use, if you currently use several), fill out the questions under that style. For each statement listed under that strategy, indicate your degree of agreement or disagreement with the statement. Then follow the instructions for calculating and interpreting your score.

If You're a *Reactor*...	Strongly Agree	Agree	Neither Agree Nor Disagree	Disagree	Strongly Disagree
1. Reflecting back over the last six months, I can think of many times when I wished I had had more control over when, how, and where I responded to a particular work or family issue.	1	2	3	4	5
2. Reflecting over the past six months, I can think of many times when I felt deep regret over my need to respond to a work or family issue on the spot.	1	2	3	4	5
3. I dislike that I often feel pulled in many different directions by my personal and work demands.	1	2	3	4	5
4. I am not getting enough sleep because my work and family demands tend to create really long days for me.	1	2	3	4	5
5. There are frequently times when people have mis-understood my availability to them, because I was focusing on an outside work or family demand.	1	2	3	4	5

If You're a *Reactor...*	Strongly Agree	Agree	Neither Agree Nor Disagree	Disagree	Strongly Disagree
6. I feel very overworked by my work and family demands as a whole, a feeling that is outweighing any positives related to how I'm managing my life.	1	2	3	4	5
7. I am less effective than I could be at work because I am constantly switching back and forth between work and family.	1	2	3	4	5
8. People sometimes see me as not committed to my work or family role because I'm constantly juggling them.	1	2	3	4	5
9. I am often interrupted much more than I would like by family matters when I am at work.	1	2	3	4	5
10. I am often interrupted much more than I would like by work matters when I am on personal time.	1	2	3	4	5
11. I would find my life more enjoyable if I were able to focus more often on one thing at a time.	1	2	3	4	5
12. I am often late for appointments because I am trying to do too much in too little time.	1	2	3	4	5
Calculating your score: Add up the total number of circles you placed in each column, and write the totals in the boxes to the right.					

Interpreting your score: If you circled "4" or "5" for most of the statements, the benefits of your style outweigh its costs, and you probably don't need to make major change. If you would still like to make small changes to improve your style, or if you circled a wide variety of numbers for the statements and you experience about equal amounts of costs and benefits for your style, consider jumping ahead to Chapter 7, "Changes Everyone Can Make to Improve Quality of Life," to make changes that can benefit everyone If you circled "1" or "2" for most of the statements, the costs of your style definitely outweigh the benefits. Besides reading Chapter 7, you also should take steps to change your Reactor strategy so that the benefits outweigh the costs. Adopting a strategy that affords you more control over how you fulfill your obligations (such as Quality Timer or Work or Family Firster) may be worth considering.

If You're a Fusion Lover...	Strongly Agree	Agree	Neither Agree Nor Disagree	Disagree	Strongly Disagree
1. Reflecting back over the last six months, I can think of many times when my style of mixing work and family caused some misunderstandings on the part of others.	1	2	3	4	5
2. Reflecting over the past six months, I can think of numerous times when my multitasking created some problems for me.	1	2	3	4	5
3. There are times when I would interact with family or friends more effectively if I could shut out work when I am doing something for my family or myself.	1	2	3	4	5
4. There are times when I would interact with colleagues or clients more effectively if I could shut out family when working.	1	2	3	4	5
5. It annoys me that some people see me as not completely committed to my job.	1	2	3	4	5
6. I would like to reduce the times when people have misunderstood my availability to them because I was focusing on an outside work or family demand.	1	2	3	4	5
7. I probably could be more productive if I weren't always switching back and forth between work and family or personal life.	1	2	3	4	5
8. At times I've had to handle work and family issues simultaneously, and this has caused confusion for other people with whom I regularly interact.	1	2	3	4	5

TRADEOFFS OF USING FLEXIBILITY FOR HIGHER WORK–LIFE INTEGRATION

If You're a Fusion Lover...	Strongly Agree	Agree	Neither Agree Nor Disagree	Disagree	Strongly Disagree
9. I would like to occasionally increase my ability to focus on just one thing at a time.	1	2	3	4	5
10. Others are often annoyed when I am interrupted by something that is unrelated (that is, when I get a personal call while at work).	1	2	3	4	5
11. I am not sure whether my way of multitasking is sustainable over the long run in my life.	1	2	3	4	5
12. Other important people in my life at family or work dislike my constant mixing of work and personal life.	1	2	3	4	5
13. I am often late for appointments because I am trying to do too much in too little time.	1	2	3	4	5
Calculating your score: Add up the total number of circles you placed in each column, and write the totals in the boxes to the right.					

Interpreting your score: If you circled "4" or "5" for most of the statements, the benefits of your style outweigh its costs, and you probably don't need to make major change. If you would still like to make small changes to improve your style, or if you circled a wide variety of numbers for the statements and you experience about equal amounts of costs and benefits for your style, consider jumping ahead to Chapter 7, "Changes Everyone Can Make to Improve Quality of Life," to make changes that can benefit everyone. If you circled "1" or "2" for most of the statements, the cost of your style definitely outweigh the benefits. Besides reading Chapter 7, you also should take steps to changing your Fusion Lover style to reduce its tradeoffs.. Refining your strategy so you blend work and nonwork commitments in ways that are more acceptable to others in your work and personal life is seriously worth considering. You might think about experimenting with the Quality Timer style and review the tradeoffs of that style to gain insight into the challenges you may face after making a change.

chapter five

Tradeoffs of Compartmentalizing Work and Personal Life

I separate for my sanity and to keep the focus on what matters most to me—my family. I enjoy my work too, and it's important to me, but if I don't set walls around it, work starts to take over everything. I feel pressure to always do my best, and so if I let work seep into the home, I end up thinking about work all the time. My daughter ends up saying things to me like "Mom, I feel like you're with me, but you're not really with me." So I try to keep work in the office and family time for family. Once the workday is done, I can shut the door to my office knowing that I've done good work and go to pick up the kids and enjoy being with them.

Elaine, Family Firster

(Elaine works out of a corporate office and makes sure to not let her work interrupt her family life when she is home.)

I write a lot of code, so it's very important for me to focus on writing....The hours that I'm working on the computer I am working for my office, and that is where I am focused.... I actually work faster than my colleagues. I am successful because I keep my work time focused in the home office and keep my family time sacred.

Tim, Work Firster

(Tim works out of a home office, with a separate door to the rest of his house and strict rules for his family about not interrupting him while working.)

Firsters: Making Your Priorities Clear Wherever You Are

Like Elaine and Tim, all Separators have a flexstyle where they try to prevent work and their personal lives from blurring together. For some, though, it's about keeping private time preserved for family first or personal life if single, whereas for others, it's about loving their work. And for still other Separators—those who are Captives—a separation flexstyle is unfortunately dictated by the fact their jobs and bosses are inflexible and won't let them work in any other way. In this chapter we share stories from all three types of Separators and examine the strengths and weaknesses of this flexstyle.

Family Firsters

When I am home, I just want to relax and play with my son. I do not want to think about work. I tend to not bring work home unless I absolutely need to.

Rosa, Family Firster

I thoroughly believe in not taking work home at all. It gets to the point where my family doesn't really know what I do. Family life is very important to me, and that time is for the family and not for work-related issues. I make a very significant effort so that I can devote the time I have for my family to my family.

Jeff, Family Firster

Meet Rosa and Jeff who are Family Firsters and generally happy and at peace with their flexstyles—at least in the short run. All of us probably know people like them and may work in this way ourselves. Family Firsters like to keep work and personal life separate because they want to be able to focus on their family or self. Unlike the Integrators we spoke with who see life as one big hyphen involving "work-family" or "work-life," Separators see "work AND family" or "work AND personal life" as divided worlds. They craft whatever decisions they make over how to structure work and family relationships in ways that enable them to devote the greatest discretionary time and energy to the family role. Protecting family life is a major psychological driver of their flexstyle. For Family Firsters, flexibility is used to maintain control over workloads and schedules to separate work from personal life psychologically, mentally, and physically. Separate buckets are created for different parts of life with work in one and personal or family life often kept in another much bigger bucket. Family Firster Separators focus on work while working, and when the day is done, they turn their attention to other things. Even though Jeff and Rosa are of different genders and life stages, they still work in the same way for similar reasons. Jeff and Rosa are both married with one child; Jeff's child is 16, and Rosa's is 1 year old. Both Jeff and Rosa work about 50 hours a week. One works for a high-technology information company, and the other works for an auto manufacturer. Both could work longer hours—most of their peers are socialized to do so at these major Fortune 100 companies. But somehow Rosa and Jeff have figured out that most people—on their deathbed when their entire life flashes before them—don't say "I wish I had spent more time working."

Ironically, although working in a plant environment creates a high degree of separation from family, some Separators like Rosa take active steps to actually increase separation between work and family life. Like Rosa, many of the people we interviewed who said they try to separate work from family and are satisfied with this way of working, do so because they place a higher identity with and value on family or personal life than work life. Although Family First Separators enjoy their jobs, they would not want a career that detracted from the personal roles of mother and wife or father and husband. These identities are of primary importance.

Being able to focus on family or personal life more easily clearly is the biggest benefit of being a Family Firster. In the current era of cell phones, pagers, and meetings set across global time zones intruding on family, these individuals not only said that family is the most important thing in their life, but they also actually made decisions to control relationships between work and personal life to keep family first. How did they do this? They learned how to say no, learned how to not over commit, and kept their eye constantly on what matters most to them in their life—their family. They also faced some tradeoffs, too.

For example, even for Family Firsters, problems occasionally arise at home that must be dealt with during work hours. Rosa tries to contain these kinds of interruptions by usually scheduling them to occur at the beginning or end of the day—as she defines it—coming into work a bit later or leaving earlier and making up the time. "This last week when I left for work, the baby was really fussy, so I came into work, finished what I had to get done for the day, and then I left early and took a half day of vacation so I could go home and be with my son." This will work fine until Rosa realizes that if she always works in this way, eventually, she may be passed up for promotions or pay raises. Also coworker, supervisor, or client relations may be negatively impacted. Someone may have needed her help and stopped by her desk, or called or e-mailed her when she was gone in the afternoon, and she never knew about it—she had worked her half day. Separators also end up taking half or full days of vacation to handle personal stuff, such as the babysitter that didn't show up, when if they had integrated a little bit they could have saved vacation time for a block of time rather than using it up in dribs and drabs.

Keep in mind that Family Firsters are not always individuals who are married with children or elder-care duties. They can be single, too. Take Stephen, who also separates work and personal life, but does so to carve out personal time for himself. He is an internal IT consultant at Datacom (pseudonym) and is unmarried without dependents. Although he works a minimal amount at home—only about 5% of his work time—even there he created a home office with a separate door and with a separate data and phone line just for work. For him, and for others like him, consciously separating is necessary to avoid work taking over his personal life. Stephen believes that regardless of whether someone is married or has children at home, it is really important for people who occasionally telecommute or work on weekends, evenings, or at times other than core work hours to learn how to set boundaries. He strives to bring as little work home as possible, even though he is starting out in his career and many others work longer hours than he does, because having some downtime for himself is important to him. He never had to work hard in high school and college and plans to continue working this way throughout his career. He also makes sure he takes a number of trips throughout the year, even during the busy season in his department, to go to New York to the theatre and to enjoy city life with his college buddies. People like Stephen—Family Firsters, but single or focused on their personal needs—often need to have space each day or week just to veg, recoup, and focus on downtime for themselves, listening to their iPod, playing Wii, or going to the gym. Others are focused on trying to be "whole" people and may value spending time with romantic partners or friends, or may devote time to church or community.

Like Rosa and Jeff, Stephen is also limiting his career by rarely working overtime and by taking off at impolitic moments. Just like those Nike commercials offering the pat advice that "image is everything," Stephen needs to remember that bosses, peers, and performance evaluations at first jobs can set the stage for his entire career in corporate life. He may not be viewed as high potential and may be let go during tough times. Like some Separators we spoke with, over time one of the biggest tradeoffs Family First Separators face is that they may not be able to develop the professional side of life as much if they continue to always work in this way over the life course. During crisis times at work, they may not be able to work the long hours needed to keep their jobs or companies afloat.

Work Firsters

Some of the same tradeoffs and dilemmas of being narrowly focused on one role also can happen to the other happy Separators we spoke with—the Work Firsters, people whose identity and values focus mainly on the work role. Achieving in the work role can be seductive——conferring money, promotions, and occupational prestige. Feedback also can be more immediate. It can take you 18 years to figure out whether you have screwed up a child from infancy. Or a decade to figure out that a marriage or partner you selected actually isn't compatible with you. Feedback at work can be as rapid as a quarterly bonus. So you may be a Work Firster now, or at other times in your life, or know someone like this. Work Firsters can be people who have trouble turning work off or shifting focus from work.

Just like the Family Firsters who may get passed over for promotions, Work Firsters can face some similar problems in the reverse for people who always put work over personal life. Over time, your family and friends may stop calling you to socialize on the weekends because they see you as less interested in forming personal relationships. And eventually this perception will become reality. People will see you only as one-sided.

Finding a balanced, rich life is challenging for Firsters—even though it is a satisfying style for some people we interviewed. If Firsters were just a little more flexible, it might help them in relationships with others. This is another important problem typically facing Firsters. Life sometimes happens in ways that cannot be segmented but have to mush together.

For example, Ralph, a business analyst, finds it difficult to easily switch roles between work and personal life. He believes he has less cognitive complexity and fewer switching costs from moving back and forth between work and family. As a Work Firster he explains: "The nature of my work can get to a high level of detail. I need to constantly check the level of thought stream with myself and others, so it is better to keep work and family life separate to help with work processes. While there are times I would really like to work at home (and my wife would like this, too, as it would really help her with the timing of her long commute if I were home earlier sometimes), but if the kids are there, there are too many distractions, and they would keep interrupting me. The separation helps me do my job better, is less stressful. (But it would be nice to try this out someday.)"

Yet someday may never come. Or when it does, the kids will be grown and Ralph's wife will have done it all, or may have left him because she got tired of always having to juggle her commute and manage the kids by herself almost like a single parent.

The Danger of Heavy Work First Styles in Time of Family Crisis

I had a friend and colleague of mine die last week of a stroke. Forty-six years old, no prior health problems, but for the last six months had been doing the work of 2 people (due to the departure of another manager and the subsequent decision not to replace him). She had been sleeping 4 hours a night. Sadly her mother passed away 6 weeks ago so she was under a tremendous amount of stress personally—and the work didn't let up. Sarah was at the office on a call when she had her stroke. She loved her job, but work became too much for her when she had a family crisis and couldn't cut back.

—Email received from a manager after a corporate training program on work and family

---

Captives

I am overwhelmed by my job and how much I have to get done each day. Usually I have no idea when my workday will end due to ongoing problems with the production line and the lack of flexibility in my work schedule. This creates a lot of conflicts for me in my personal life. I never know when I will get home. What gets to me the most is that I don't sit down to dinner some nights until 9:00 p.m. I don't even have time to do my laundry or clean my house sometimes. And I really need this job. The economy is bad, and [the job] pays well. Where else could I go at this stage of my life?

Paul, Captive

Not every Separator we spoke with was happy. Those who are Captives—individuals forced to separate their job and personal life like Paul—are dissatisfied with this arrangement. What we found and what we hope you will understand as you take this journey to become the CEO of you and manage your flexstyle better is that it is not as important *what* flexstyle people are enacting, but *how* and *why* they are doing it. And most important is *whether they feel good or at peace* with their life. Do they see their life as generally working well? Are they living the life they wanted that fits with their hopes and dreams for their desired allocation of life buckets?

Captives may be living their lives similarly to Work Firsters, but they feel badly about it. They are unhappy. On paper their flexstyles may look similar. They may even appreciate some of the benefits that all Separators enjoy: They have clarity about what role they focus on at any given time, and they don't have the stress of shifting roles all the time. But for Captives, these benefits are vastly outweighed by the downsides of their style and particularly by their limited ability to address their personal needs. Captives can be good employees and highly involved in their work. They just need a little more control to be able to have a bit of a personal life.

Take Paul who is a materials manager. When Paul was asked how significant his job is in respect to its impact on other people in the organization and their ability to perform their jobs, he answered highly significant. He knows that if he does not perform his job competently and efficiently, others in the organization will be unable to do their jobs. This responsibility is taken seriously by Paul and is one of the aspects of his job that he enjoys: "I like it that my job is important, but because it is I feel responsible even when I am not at work." What does not come with his job is autonomy.

When asked how much control or say he has in regard to how, when, or where his job is performed, Paul told us that he has little to no personal say. This is an aspect that he does not like about his position. Paul desires the ability to rearrange some of the tasks he currently performs in the office to better balance his work-life roles. Many of the phone calls and paper work that must be completed on a daily basis in the office, he feels could be done just as well at his home. "I would like to be able to do some of my work at home. It would really cut down on the long days spent at work. A lot of my work is calling suppliers to check on schedules. I could do this at home."

By performing some of the tedious tasks at home, Paul believes he could better balance his work-life roles. One of the issues that Paul has with his current job is the inability to perform his daily household chores such as laundry or mowing the lawn. By making phone calls from his home, he would be able to multitask. This would allow Paul more time to spend with his family and friends. When he becomes overloaded by work and home roles, Paul responds by shutting down and is not capable of completing any tasks. "When I get really busy, I cannot focus. I end up shutting down, and I can't get anything done. This is the worst. If I could incorporate some of my work at home, it would be better for me." Paul then goes on to say, "I know this sounds strange, but if I was able to bring work home, I think I would be able to separate work-life roles in a positive way. It would give me more time and that way when I am with family, I would not be distracted by work. If I had more time outside of work, I would feel better about my life."

In sum, Captives face different tradeoffs than Firsters. They have more stress, because unlike Firsters they perceive that they lack control over how and when they do their jobs and manage their lives. They are dissatisfied with their overall quality of life. They also have less time and energy to devote to their personal life and may feel burned out and ultimately pay deep personal costs for their captivity. They may become overweight, depressed, or addicted to alcohol or overeating, and have few friends or positive personal relationships with family. The flexstyle their jobs make them follow is not sustainable.

Table 5.1 summarizes some of the tradeoffs of the Separator flexstyles.

Table 5.1 *Summary of Tradeoffs of Separators*

		Advantages	Disadvantages
Separation Styles	Firsters (Work or Family)	Focus on valued roles	Miss key work or life events
		Signal limits of one's availability to boss, clients, and coworkers, or to family and friends	Possible negative coworker, client, or supervisor reactions
			Negative career impacts for family-first Separators
		Reduce stress (from switching between work and family)	Lack of work-family cross-domain support (e.g., lack of support for family from work resources, or lack of support for work from family resources)
	Captives	Focus on work roles	Miss key family and life events
		Signal limits of one's availability to nonwork others	Role conflict and stress
			Less developed nonwork life
		Reduce stress (from switching)	Families/friends can become short-changed or victims of our work demands
			Lack of work-family cross-domain support

You may have seen yourself in a number of the stories we have told. Overall, the biggest tradeoffs for Firsters are fourfold:

- **Stunted personal, community, and family life.** Because Separators do not adjust their work hours to accommodate demands from other dimensions of their lives, they risk missing out on valued experiences from those dimensions. For example, we spoke with people like Thomas, who works a strict eight-hour day at his employer's office and feels he can't take the afternoon off to see his parents when they phone to say they'll be in town unexpectedly that afternoon. Or Sarah, who wants to participate in her town's civic organization, but regretfully declines when she learns that the club meetings are held at noontime on Mondays—when she's at work and can't take time to drive to the meetings—even though she actually could if she wanted to.

- **Lack of access to cross-domain enrichment[1] and supports.** Separation also means that Firsters and Captives miss out on positive enrichment that can occur between work and personal life. Telling your spouse or friend about positive experiences at work can increase the impact for you—even in just small ways such as by making you feel even better about the event. Work colleagues, if they know about a personal stress you are having, can sometimes assist. Take Stephanie: When her husband became ill, she was surprised when several of her colleagues stopped by to bring food and offer some comfort. There can be benefits to sharing across domains, and Separators miss out on these potential benefits.

  This is an example of one of the downsides of separating. Because Firsters are trying to not discuss work issues when at home or family or personal life issues with close friends at work, they lack access to information and social support that Integrators and Volleyers have. Yet many problems related to work and life cross borders between these worlds. Sometimes discussing difficulties occurring in one life domain when in the other provides extra resources to help resolve issues and give new perspectives on these matters. Many Separators' families do not know a lot about their jobs, and their coworkers do not know a lot about their families, which limits networks of access to critical knowledge on how to solve problems at work or at home.

- **Professional Stigma (for Family Firsters).** In organizations that want employees to always be available, a working person's boss and colleagues may stigmatize Family Firsters. Consider Wendy, who arrived at a 32-hour-week arrangement with her employer by which she works four 8-hour days, Monday through Thursday. She negotiated this arrangement, including taking a pay cut, so she could focus entirely on nonwork interests—including community projects and music lessons—on Fridays. Yet her company has an unspoken norm of unpaid overtime. So Wendy has ended up working four 10-hour days—8 hours of which she doesn't get paid for—to stave off complaints from coworkers who conclude she's not working as hard as they are. Occasionally, coworkers have expressed annoyance that Wendy won't make an exception to her Friday off rule to help out on a crucial deadline.

  In addition to working unpaid time, Wendy worries that negative attitudes toward flexible work arrangements at her firm will mean she'll miss out on promotions. Her concern is well founded: In many companies, people who have made it clear that their job isn't their only priority are passed over when valuable opportunities arise—whether it's a promotion, a chance to participate in a key project, or the opportunity to work on a cross-functional team.

- **Stunted/UnHealthy Social Life (for Work Firsters).** Like Family Firsters, Work Firsters are also stigmatized, just in the reverse in their social life. They may have fewer friends than other flexstyles, because they have over the years invested very little in their social life. Or they have turned down so many social invitations people stop asking. They also may find it difficult to exercise and take care of their image, which creates a vicious cycle where they may look shabby and unhealthy, thereby limiting their social appeal.

We must note that Captives face the biggest challenges because of their lack of control and lack of happiness with their style:

Special Considerations for Captives

For decades, many academics who study work-life issues have argued that separating work and home is a flawed approach because it puts people in positions of terrible role conflict where they feel stressed and pulled apart by competing demands of their home and work. This idea grew from research that showed that workers in traditional jobs suffered because they wanted to deal with personal issues from time to time but were prevented from doing so by the nature of their jobs, by unsupportive work cultures, and by the management in their organizations.[2] These findings are echoed in the experiences of workers we spoke with who are Captives. Being forced to separate—to act as if you are only a worker in work hours when in your heart you would rather work flexible hours so that you could take care of personal matters, such as taking your spouse or child to medical appointments—can cause long-term role conflict, stress, and unhappiness.

Overall, the biggest difficulty Captives face is they lack control over work hours and schedules. They also lack sufficient power to make change to a different flexstyle without being forced to change jobs, employers, or their personal family situation. There are no upsides to being a Captive, except that if you are someone who likes to have your life structured for you, you don't have to make decisions on whether and how to integrate work and life. These decisions have been made for you based on the structure of your job or family.

We hope in the change chapters that follow, Captives can use both general and specific tips we will share to get more control and choice—even if within the smallest margins of their job—over how to change their flexstyles.

The following section contains some assessments to help you weigh the tradeoffs in your life. Fill out only the section that fits your style—if you are a Captive or a Firster. If you are a Work Firster, think about the questions in terms of placing work over other personal commitments. If you are a Family Firster, think about the questions in terms of placing family or personal life over professional commitments.

For Separators: Weighing the Tradeoffs in Your Life

Instructions: Select the flexstyle that most resembles the one you use (or primarily use, if you currently use several). For each statement listed under that strategy, indicate your degree of agreement or disagreement with the statement. Then follow the instructions for calculating and interpreting your score.

Separator Strategies

If You're a *Firster* (Work or Family)...	Strongly Agree	Agree	Neither Agree Nor Disagree	Disagree	Strongly Disagree
1. Reflecting back over the last six months, I can think of numerous times when I wished I had more time or energy to devote to either my work or personal life.	1	2	3	4	5
2. Reflecting over the past six months, I can think of numerous times when I deeply regretted making my work or personal life a priority over the other.	1	2	3	4	5
3. It has created problems for my career or family well-being that I have had to make sacrifices to be able to focus on either my personal or my professional life over the other one.	1	2	3	4	5
4. I don't live a well-rounded life that I find effectively balances personal and professional identities.	1	2	3	4	5
5. People whose opinions I value would like me to have a more flexible way to handle the priorities in my life.	1	2	3	4	5
6. I feel stigmatized sometimes by others over the choices I have made to focus on either work or family/personal life, and this feeling bothers me.	1	2	3	4	5
7. I am dissatisfied with focusing so much on mainly one part of my life (either my career over my family or my family over my career).	1	2	3	4	5
8. I find myself dreaming of a richer existence in which I have more time for a number of interests.	1	2	3	4	5

If You're a *Firster* (Work or Family)...	Strongly Agree	Agree	Neither Agree Nor Disagree	Disagree	Strongly Disagree
9. I believe I have been passed over at times for inclusion in either personal or professional opportunities because the people in charge of those opportunities see me as one-dimensional.	1	2	3	4	5
10. I feel that I'm living a stunted life, and I would like to explore new ways of managing professional and personal demands.	1	2	3	4	5
11. I wish that the tradeoffs between work and family were not so black and white.	1	2	3	4	5
12. I am dissatisfied that I do not have an equally developed work and personal life.	1	2	3	4	5
Calculating your score: Add up the total number of circles you placed in each column and write the totals in the boxes to the right.					

Interpreting your score: If you circled "4" or "5" for most of the statements, the benefits of your style outweigh its costs, and you probably don't need to make major change. If you would still like to make small changes to improve your style, or if you circled a wide variety of numbers for the statements and you experience about equal amounts of costs and benefits for your style, consider jumping ahead to Chapter 7, "Changes Everyone Can Make to Improve Quality of Life," to make changes that can benefit everyone. If you circled "1" or "2" for most of the statements, the costs of your style definitely outweigh the benefits. Besides reading Chapter 7, you also should explore making small changes to more effectively allocate your time and energy to your priorities. You also may want to experiment with other flexstyles, such as Quality Timer.

If You're a *Captive*...	Strongly Agree	Agree	Neither Agree Nor Disagree	Disagree	Strongly Disagree
1. Reflecting back over the last six months, I can think of numerous times when my inability to flexibly manage work and personal life created big problems for me.	1	2	3	4	5

If You're a *Captive*...	Strongly Agree	Agree	Neither Agree Nor Disagree	Disagree	Strongly Disagree
2. Reflecting over the past six months, I can think of numerous times when my having limited ability to control how I blend work and personal demands created some problems for me.	1	2	3	4	5
3. I feel highly frustrated by the inflexibility of the way I'm currently managing my work and home life.	1	2	3	4	5
4. I must find a more flexible way to manage work and personal life.	1	2	3	4	5
5. I am severely depressed by the current rigidity in my life.	1	2	3	4	5
6. I need to find a new way of living that gives me more choices over how to juggle work and personal life.	1	2	3	4	5
7. I feel trapped by my current job and family structure.	1	2	3	4	5
8. I feel burned out by my current life situation.	1	2	3	4	5
9. I want more control over when and where I manage work and personal responsibilities throughout the week.	1	2	3	4	5
10. I strongly dislike the lack of choice I have in how I manage work and personal life relationships.	1	2	3	4	5
Calculating your score: Add up the total number of circles you placed in each column and write the totals in the boxes to the right.					

Interpreting your score: If you circled "4" or "5" for most of the statements, the benefits of your style outweigh its costs, and you probably don't need to make major change. If you would still like to make small changes to improve your style, or if you circled a wide variety of numbers for the statements and you experience about equal amounts of costs and benefits for your style, consider jumping ahead to Chapter 7, "Changes Everyone Can Make to Improve Quality of Life," to make changes that can benefit everyone. If you circled "1" or "2" for most of the statements, the costs of your style definitely outweigh the benefits. Besides reading Chapter 7, you also may want to reshape your flexstyle so that it gives you more control over how you manage your priorities. You might consider adopting a Quality Timer, Work or Family Firster, or Fusion Lover approach.

chapter six

Tradeoffs of Volleying Between Separating and Integrating

When I got out of graduate school, I joined a big Fortune 500 firm and was lucky enough to land a job near my husband's graduate program in the East. Then it was his turn, and he took at job on the West Coast, and for a while my employer was more than happy to let me work virtually after we moved to Seattle since I was a top performer. That was great for my husband and me in our early years of marriage. I was working from home, and he was establishing his career. Then, after a year or so, my company made it clear I had to pick a new major site to work at somewhere on the West Coast. My husband and I didn't want me to commute or move so that's when I left the company. If I hadn't left the company, my career would have probably stalled since there weren't many people working virtually at the time. Fortunately, I had a good headhunter and a great resume, so I was easily able to land a job with a high-technology company that was rapidly growing. After working at the new firm for a while and getting constant promotions, by my late thirties, I had risen to the executive level. I am now one of the only senior women at the highest ranks. I am a VP and report to the president. My employer promoted me right after I had my second child and had been back on the job only a short time.

My husband kept telling me how smart he thought my boss was to do that—to promote me right after the birth of my second child. My boss knew I was vulnerable at that time in my life because I was wavering on how hard I wanted to work on the fast track with a second newborn that I had waited a long time to have. Since he gave me such a great promotion, there was no way I was going to quit or cut back, but something had to give, because of the two young kids we had at home. With my career clearly in high gear, we decided my husband would work from home on a reduced load schedule, which suits him and our family perfectly. I am able to focus on work and regularly travel overseas to our global operations.

Even though I work 60 to 70 hours a week, I feel blessed and couldn't be happier with my life. When I am home, I try to not do much work, and my weekends are special to our family so except during peak work periods (which seem to be more and more lately!)...I have a short commute except when I have global travel, a happy marriage, and kids I love. Life is good.

Things run smoothly for providing the care for our now two school-age children, because my husband is always there to keep the house going. If there's something important going on for the kids, I'll sometimes mix things up a bit, bringing work home so I can stay involved. When I'm in town, I'm one of those parents you might see checking e-mail on my Blackberry during the championship soccer game. I try to make the major school or sports events. But often my husband manages the day-to-day stuff. He is highly focused and productive at working out of our home, and his employer knows they are getting a good deal—a top researcher at a slight pay discount. If I hadn't taken the risk to leave my old, more traditional company, or married a partner who wasn't willing to adjust to support me, I doubt I would be leading the wonderful life I am now.

Still sometimes when I have time to stop and think about my life so far, I feel a little nagging sadness. I wish that I could have had my kids a little earlier in my career when it wasn't in such hyper drive and could have been able to spend more time with them when they were little. Even now I would love to be able to cut back a little more to spend more time with them, as before I know it they will be going off to college. Over the past year, I have usually been able to block off Friday afternoons and make no meetings so I can be at home and spend some quality time with the kids. That has been absolutely huge for me psychologically and provides special time—not like when we are rushing during most of the week.

Lately it has been harder and harder to protect even these few hours of quality time. Increasingly I have had difficulty being able to leave the office a little early even on Fridays or being able to protect weekend time for family. My career has really taken off so much that with all the stock options I have, I feel a little trapped in my breadwinner role, and frankly it sometimes gets exhausting always having to work so hard to carve out quality time. And then there are times I have taken off early on a Friday, and the kids have ended up having sports practice or other activities, so I haven't been able to do anything with them anyway, so it is getting frustrating trying to figure out how to create those special family moments regularly throughout a week.

Sarah, VP at a high-technology firm

Sarah's Story: Striving to Protect "Quality Time"

Volleyers have defined periods of their lives, times of the year, or workweeks where they switch back and forth and at times experience work and life as tightly demarcated from each other, like when Sarah is spending her Friday afternoons at home, and at other times mix all aspects of their life. Sarah's job is so demanding that even though she sets her own schedule and can control her calendar, she is not the kind of person who makes it to every little family event, just the big ones. She does more integrating of work into family than the reverse, and though she can have quality time because she is a respected senior manager, she does have to separate for periods each week due to the nature of her job. Just like the other flexstyles for how people manage work and personal life, there are usually two main subgroups where one group is generally happy and in control, and the other group is unhappy, not in control, and their values are compromised. If you're a Volleyer or someone you know is, hopefully you or they are in the subgroup of people who usually feel in control and at peace—the Quality Timers like Sarah—and not the other clusters—the Job Warriors, where job demands or travel keep creeping into precious personal and family time.

The main downsides that both Quality Timers and Job Warriors share as Volleyers are the ever-constant problem of *job creep*—where work creeps into personal time—and the heightened cognitive complexity of making family and work systems mesh well together in a constantly shifting constellation of life configurations. In this chapter we give illustrations of these subgroups and some examples of how Volleyers work hard to make their lives work effectively. Managing work and family is a constant focus of this group—almost like a third major life task. Doing one's job is in one bucket, managing one's personal life to ensure quality time or attend to family demands is in another, and the third bucket is figuring out how to make everything mesh and blend well together.

Quality Timers' Tradeoffs and Strategies for Making Life Work

> The master in the art of living makes little distinction between his work and his play, his labor and his leisure, his mind and his body, his education and his recreation, his love and his religion. He hardly knows which is which. He simply pursues his vision of excellence in whatever he does, leaving others to decide whether he is working or playing. To him, he is always doing both.
>
> Zen Buddhist from "Head to Head" by Lester Thurow, NY; Warner Books, 1992

Even Quality Timer Volleyers—those individuals who are generally happy being able to focus sometimes more on the family and sometimes more on work with periods of mixing these worlds—also must grapple with unique challenges in implementing their flexstyles effectively.

To organize their lives in ways that enable them to shift from one approach to another, many Volleyers feel they must establish routines and structures that can ultimately prove complex and elaborate or inflexible. Early in her career, Sarah was a happy Fusion Lover. Her life was simple then. She had just gotten married and was working from home for a major firm. Her career was equal or secondary to her husband's. Now she is becoming a superstar, and she is desperately trying to hold onto her quality time approach at the same time her career is pushing her to work more and more hours. Her strategy to block off Friday afternoons is a great idea, but it is getting harder to protect and more impractical to carry out without her employer's support and without cutting back the workload. Now that her husband and kids have developed systems that work well without her, it is sometimes difficult to make the time she has off mesh with their "free time" and make that quality time magically happen on cue.

One challenge for Quality Timers is that it truly is a balancing act to keep everything under control and working well. It can be easy to slip off the balance beam and quickly become a Job Warrior—where work is structuring your life, particularly when you are in a major organizational contributor role or on the fast track. It takes true thoughtfulness and work to make quality time actually work. Take Marian's approach to managing quality time.

Marian: Managing Family Like a Business

Marian is an information technology consultant for the retail industry. A Quality Timer, she has worked hard to craft a life that's satisfying on all fronts. In her previous job, she had to travel three days a week for three weeks out of every month. She left the company because she, her husband, and her growing family began to resent her extensive travel.

Now she has a much more comfortable situation. For two days a week, she works onsite at customers' facilities as a subcontractor for her client, a Fortune 100 firm. Her job is to help customers manage their supply chains. She works in customer facilities from 8:00 a.m. to 3:00 p.m. one day and from 8:00 a.m. to

4:00 p.m. the second day. According to Marian, her client prefers this arrangement because "they believe that having you onsite keeps you more informed." While she's at customer facilities, Marian separates personal from professional life: She focuses solely on work during the day. Then, when she returns home, she leaves the workday behind and gives all her attention to her family and other personal commitments.

During the remaining three days of the workweek, Marian both separates and integrates. She works from home on those days—making her two children breakfast before they head off to school and giving them a snack after school. She focuses on work during the day but also works a little in the evenings if she decides that doing so is necessary to meet a deadline or solve a thorny work problem. However, she tries to keep integrating to a minimum. As she puts it, "[If colleagues or customers call you at home and] you have a screaming baby or [barking] dog in the background, people get uncomfortable and irritated by it and will tend to favor calling your peers or others for similar information. I've seen it happen to others."

To navigate the shifts between integrating and separating work and personal life, Marian works closely with her husband to establish structures for managing their many commitments. For example, at the beginning of the week, she and her husband compare their schedules and decide who will handle which family responsibilities. On Sunday night, Marian defines work and family goals for the coming week. She also pays household bills that evening. If she has to travel, her husband takes their younger child to daycare when it opens at 7:30 a.m., as he doesn't have to arrive at the office until 9:00 in the morning. If he needs to go to work earlier on a day when Marian can't bring the child to daycare, he enlists a neighbor or his mother-in-law. Marian limits her business travel to one or two overnights by flying out at 6:00 a.m. and flying home late at night. Her eldest child, a 12-year-old girl, pitches in by taking responsibility for getting herself to the school bus every morning by 7:00 a.m. Marian explains: "[Making sure these arrangements succeed] takes discipline and [it means] being task focused for both work and family."

Marian prefers to separate most of the time, integrating only when there's no other option. The sturdy support system she has developed with her spouse, mother, and friends enables her to avoid the strain and distraction that can come with tackling professional and family responsibilities simultaneously. The ability to telecommute allows her to mix work and family on the relatively rare occasions when she needs to. She has also developed agreements with her client that further help her separate. In particular, she has made it clear that she prefers not to take work-related phone calls or handle extensive job responsibilities after her designated work hours. Her client gets value in return for this arrangement: While she's on the job, she devotes all of her attention to the work and avoids handling family issues.

As a successful independent consultant who has adopted a disciplined flexstyle, Marian calls the shots in terms of how she fulfills career and family commitments. Yet maintaining her control requires careful planning, as well as the willingness to be flexible. For Marian, it also means treating her family and home life as she would a business. As she puts it, "Things work and our family is balanced because we have managed to balance the family 'business'—if that makes sense."

For example, she and her husband have decided to get out of debt and live within their means, a move that they feel certain will give them much more freedom to run their work and family lives in ways they want. They have also established a firm set of rules for managing the family and household as a business. See the following shaded box "Managing the Family Business" for details. According to Marian, the keys to managing family and household commitments are the same as those required to manage one's career: "Love what you do, respect who you work [or live] with, be honest, and communicate. If you [do] those things, the rest [falls into place]."

Managing the Family Business
1. Communicate with your spouse or partner every weekend about the upcoming week's priorities, work schedules, and outside activities. Sit down with the whole family and develop a schedule for the week that incorporates everyone's commitments. Jointly work through any conflicts.
2. Share household responsibilities, dividing them according to who does which chores best.

3. Determine your children's most pressing needs—for example, an hour a week talking with teachers at the school, or being home when they get home. Create a plan that enables you to fulfill those needs reliably.

4. Explain to your children that you work because you love them and want to provide for them as well as yourself, sometimes. But reassure them that you will still meet all their important needs.

5. Keep your family business in order. Determine who is best at managing day-to-day household financial matters. At least once a month, discuss the household's financial health and work out ways to address problems.

6. Identify meaningful or fun activities in which the whole family can participate, such as church on Wednesday night or Saturday afternoon movies at home.

7. Respect the schedules of the individuals who provide you with childcare backup. For example, as soon as you know about an upcoming business trip, contact members of your support network and make arrangements for coverage.

8. Have a conversation with your family on what is most meaningful and tradeoffs and compromises (for example, smaller house, slower promotions, and so on).

Clearly, even with the extensive control Marian has over how she manages her life, her strategy requires significant investments in coordination, communication, and planning. Not all of us are as together as Marian and could make this flexstyle work or not creep into the Job Warrior flexstyle where the job creeps into and takes more and more of personal time.

Most Volleyers have far less control or discipline than Marian to run such tight work and home ships. The following profile of Jeff sheds additional light on how difficult volleying can be when the job simply won't relax its grip.

Jeff: Travel Strains

Jeff is a project manager. He travels frequently and lives in a corporate apartment Monday through Thursday. Jeff believes he has little choice about separating his family and work on the four days per week that he is traveling, and so tries to regain some control and to integrate on his terms on the few days that he works at home. When he isn't on the road, he works from a home office, and he could close himself off from his family. His home office has a separate entrance and a door that separates the space from the rest of the living area. He also has access to a data line, phone line, computer, and e-mail that are exclusively used for work purposes. But, while he is largely focused on work at home, he also integrates so that he can pay more attention to home chores and other family needs.

He says, "On the day(s) that I am home I can take care of personal obligations that cannot be done on the weekend. Also, if I can get the work done around the house during the day, then I will actually have the weekend to spend with my family. Being gone four days a week, being able to spend time with family doing fun stuff instead of doing work stuff is important."

Although Jeff finds that being a Job Warrior on the road isn't all bad, it also can be tiring to travel so much, and it is difficult to be away when something comes up at home. On a recent trip, it seemed to Jeff like everything went wrong. His wife is used to juggling her job and taking care of their daughter, Haley, when he is away, but she was particularly stressed on this trip because they were renovating their house, and she didn't like having to deal with the contractors and issues that inevitably arose. Then the cat went missing, Haley got the stomach flu, and Jeff felt guilty and frustrated about being away and unable to pitch in. He worked extra hard to try to finish early and get back to his corporate apartment to at least talk to his wife, but usually ended up having to work full days and then stay up late nights on the phone talking things through with his wife. After arriving home exhausted, he wanted nothing more than a break and time to unwind, but he had to help his wife with all the tasks that had piled up in his absence. His Friday for working at home, which often is a relaxing day in which he likes to do an errand or two around his work, instead this time was a blur of taking care of his daughter, calls to contractors, and so little work that it spilled over to the weekend. Before he knew it, he was heading for the airport to leave again. Not every week is this hectic and stressful for Jeff and his family, but at times like this, having travel dictate when he can separate or integrate his professional and personal activities is a strain.

Volleying poses several other challenges for both Quality Timers and Job Warriors. Consider these examples:

- **Difficulty prioritizing.** Many Volleyers become confused about which demands—work or nonwork—are more pressing at a particular moment. As a result, they end up pursuing both types of demands in a haphazard way, putting themselves at risk of delivering mediocre performance on each.

- **Others' role confusion.** Like Integrators, Volleyers may unwittingly convey confusing messages about their roles and availability to colleagues, family members, or friends. For instance, suppose Larry, who works from a home office, usually mixes work and community responsibilities during the day but occasionally compartmentalizes them when he needs to concentrate on a particularly difficult work project. When he needs to compartmentalize, neighbors and friends with whom he's collaborating on a community initiative may have difficulty understanding his annoyed reaction when they phone him or drop in unannounced. After all, most of the time he doesn't seem to mind taking a break during the workday to tackle neighborhood projects. Result? They begin questioning his commitment.

Special Considerations for Job Warriors

- **Fatigue.** Volleyers who have jobs characterized by extensive travel or long hours working each week are particularly at risk for exhaustion. They also face the problem of having to jointly manage face time at the office while handling personal responsibilities—from the car needing an oil change to calling an elderly relative's doctor to discuss medical needs. Many of the people we spoke with who travel a lot for business integrate work and personal life during the few days a week they are not traveling not as a choice but because those days represent their only hope of having a personal or family life.

  Even on the weekend, Job Warriors who travel face problems unwinding. Some people we spoke with try to separate on the weekends. They try not to do any work and try to take a break and compensate for the time away to focus solely on partners or children, or even just to sleep in. But many individuals are too tired from traveling or working excessive hours even if not out of town. They were often overloaded by handling all the personal stuff that must get done in any given week. Then on the weekend they must tackle household chores such as mowing the lawn or going to an after hours clinic if they or another family member get sick. There is often little left of themselves to offer family or friends in the way of energy, enthusiasm, and attention.

Job warriors who don't have families may have stunted personal lives. They have little energy to devote to private interests, community projects, or other nonwork endeavors. And they also face the additional challenge of trying to create a personal life and develop a family. There just isn't enough time, energy, or opportunity.

- **Cognitive complexity.** Job Warriors—especially those who travel—endure an extra level of stress that comes with working regularly from a multitude of locations, including a home office; a corporate office; the plane, bus, or train while traveling; and the car while commuting. Each of these locations requires different routines and tactics for using the computer and other equipment. The varied locations may also present an array of obstacles to getting the job done—everything from an airplane seatmate who takes up more than his share of elbow room to a consistently harrowing commute that makes it impossible to sustain a cell phone conversation with a boss or colleague. Surmounting this hodge-podge of obstacles can wear down even the most energized worker.

- **Vulnerability to breakdown of support system.** Volleying strategies, particularly the Job Warrior approach, often require an extensive support system—such as a spouse and a network of neighbors, relatives, and friends who are willing and able to pitch in while you're traveling. Thus, users of such strategies are highly vulnerable to any breakdown in that support system, whether it's a reliable neighbor who suddenly moves away or a spouse who decides to leave because he or she is fed up with the working person's lack of availability.

Table 6.1 summarizes the tradeoffs of the Volleyers flexstyle.

Table **6.1** *Summary of Tradeoffs of Volleyers*

Summary		Pros	Cons
Volleyers Tradeoffs	Quality Timer	Flexibility and ability to adjust attention to most pressing work or life concern Full engagement in work and family Ability to advance family and career at the same time	Sometimes can face confusion over which demands are more pressing and may end up pursuing both work and nonwork life in middle-of-the-road way and at risk for mediocre outcomes for both Role confusion possible for family and coworkers
	Job Warriors	Ability to focus on each role when physically there Ability to have some down-time on weekends Ability to have some quiet time for self on the road at end of the day Can increase appreciation from family and friends when available Ability to sometimes change jobs or have new career experiences yet keep family or personal life stable	Fatigue Overloaded weekends spent on mundane household tasks that workers with more flexible schedules can do in the week Miss life and work events happening during the week Vulnerable to breakdown of support system; may not work for someone who lacks a partner who can pitch hit while you are on the road Sunday night blues as leaving for road or another grinding long workweek
Challenges all Volleyers face: Job creep Increased cognitive complexity Difficulty setting priorities or often must choose between work and personal life Role confusion			

For Volleyers: Weighing the Tradeoffs in Your Life

If you are a Volleyer, you may now want to pause to fill out the following self-assessment to gauge whether you are benefiting from the current way you manage relationships between work and home.

Volleyers' Strategies

If You're a Job Warrior...	Strongly Agree	Agree	Neither Agree Nor Disagree	Disagree	Strongly Disagree
1. Reflecting back over the last six months, I can think of numerous times when I wished I had had more control over when I had to either travel or have heavy peak work demands.	1	2	3	4	5
2. Reflecting over the past six months, I can think of numerous times when I deeply regretted being physically unavailable for a family or personal need.	1	2	3	4	5
3. I am often too tired to focus on my family when I am home because I am spending too much time working on my job due to travel or too high a workload.	1	2	3	4	5
4. It creates problems for those I care about in my personal life because my job is structured such that there are periods when I have to handle all of my family or personal issues in a compressed time.	1	2	3	4	5
5. My family sometimes doesn't understand that I need time just to relax when I get back from working on a major job project or a business trip.	1	2	3	4	5
6. Scheduling appointments is a real problem for me, because I never know when I will be in town or able to take off work.	1	2	3	4	5

If You're a *Job Warrior...*	Strongly Agree	Agree	Neither Agree Nor Disagree	Disagree	Strongly Disagree
7. My long hours spent at work, either traveling or working in the office, are sometimes misinterpreted by my family and friends as not caring about what goes on outside my job.	1	2	3	4	5
8. I am getting out of shape from spending so much time on work; I have not had enough time to take care of myself or my home.	1	2	3	4	5
9. My heavy periods of high workload or frequent travel often create problems in my personal life.	1	2	3	4	5
10. I dislike having to squeeze in all personal and family tasks during certain times of the week or certain times of the year when I am not traveling or working long hours on the job.	1	2	3	4	5
11. When I am on the road or in a heavy workload situation and something needs to get done for my family or at home, I have no backup, which is a severe problem.	1	2	3	4	5
Calculating your score: Add up the total number of circles you placed in each column, and write the totals in the boxes to the right.					

Interpreting your score: If you circled "4" or "5" for most of the statements, the benefits of your style outweigh its costs, and you probably don't need to make major change. If you would still like to make small changes to improve your style, or if you circled a wide variety of numbers for the statements and you experience about equal amounts of costs and benefits for your style, consider jumping ahead to Chapter 7, "Changes Everyone Can Make to Improve Quality of Life," to make changes that can benefit everyone. If you circled "1" or "2" for most of the statements, the costs of your style definitely outweigh the benefits. Besides reading Chapter 7, you may want to experiment with a flexstyle that gives you more control over how you're managing your life (such as Fusion Lover, Quality Timer, or Work or Family Firster).

Volleyers' Strategies (continued)

If You're a *Quality Timer...*	Strongly Agree	Agree	Neither Agree Nor Disagree	Disagree	Strongly Disagree
1. Reflecting back over the last six months, I can think of numerous times when I wished I didn't have to devote so much energy to ensuring I had enough quality time for my job or my family.	1	2	3	4	5
2. Reflecting over the past six months, I can think of numerous times when I regretted that the way I draw the line between work and family feels like a delicate balancing act.	1	2	3	4	5
3. Although I generally do a good job of juggling work and family, I often feel like things could easily fall apart.	1	2	3	4	5
4. I feel a lot of pressure to manage relationships between work and family in an ideal way.	1	2	3	4	5
5. I am not sure how sustainable my quality-time style is over the long run—it feels like something will have to give.	1	2	3	4	5
6. It might be better for me to be able to fully focus on work some of the time and family some of the time at different times of the year or week.	1	2	3	4	5
7. People think I have the perfect life, but they don't know how hard I have to work to juggle my job and family well.	1	2	3	4	5

If You're a *Quality Timer...*	Strongly Agree	Agree	Neither Agree Nor Disagree	Disagree	Strongly Disagree
8. At times I would like to be able to multitask more, because it would help me miss out less on things that matter to me.	1	2	3	4	5
9. The idea of quality time sounds good in theory, but I know it is not a realistic strategy for the long run.	1	2	3	4	5
10. I would like to explore new ways of improving how I am balancing work and personal life.	1	2	3	4	5
11. Although sometimes I can control how much I blend boundaries between work and personal life, I sometimes regret not being able to focus on one area over another.	1	2	3	4	5
Calculating your score: Add up the total number of circles you placed in each column, and write the totals in the boxes to the right.					

Interpreting your score: If you circled "4" or "5" for most of the statements, the benefits of your style outweigh its costs, and you probably don't need to make major change. If you would still like to make small changes to improve your style, or if you circled a wide variety of numbers for the statements and you experience about equal amounts of costs and benefits for your style, consider jumping ahead to Chapter 7, "Changes Everyone Can Make to Improve Quality of Life," to make changes that can benefit everyone. If you circled "1" or "2" for most of the statements, the costs of your style definitely outweigh the benefits. Besides reading Chapter 7, you may want to consider making some incremental changes that enable you to better carve out quality time for your job or family in a way that is seen as more effective by others you care about. You may want to experiment with a Work or Family Firster strategy, or a Fusion Lover approach, at some point in the future.

Changes Everyone Can Make to Improve Quality of Life

I have been on a personal growth path over the last few years and have learned a tremendous amount. Finding a partner I wanted to be with more than working makes me think about how to have my personal life be a bigger part of each day. It triggered new reflection and motivation to get out of my rut. Since I have made changes in my life to allow me to better jointly accommodate my work and personal goals, I am so much more at peace. I am now a much different person in terms of having grown personally and professionally. It was scary at first, but I am glad I took the risk and improved how I was living each day so that I am more in control and have a richer life.

Small Steps You Can Take to Begin to Gain Control

This chapter focuses on changes you can make to gain control and be CEO of your own life, regardless of which flexstyle you now have. Take Cindy, a professional who always excelled at her career. After years of putting her work ahead of her personal life and seeing all her friends get married and start families before she did, Cindy finally met someone who was her equal and became engaged. Recently she relocated to the city where her fiancé has a new job, and to make this move, she had to shift from working at a regular office to telecommuting. Cindy, who had always drawn tight lines between her job and her personal life, decided that because she was working at home, she would experiment with a flexstyle that is much higher on mixing work and personal life throughout the day. Before she knew it, she was breaking up her work day with phone calls to make wedding arrangements and with trips to the market to get supplies for dinner. She thought she'd always be able to make up the time but found it didn't work out quite how she anticipated. "I knew things were bad when I caught myself one afternoon having a lunch that morphed into a three-hour break as I met with the wedding planner for the eighth time in the past few months."

She also had a creeping suspicion that she was being forgotten at corporate, because she periodically discovered she'd been left out of some conference calls and projects for new business. Cindy talked to her supervisor and her fiancé about how to make things better. She first negotiated to work out of a satellite office instead of telecommuting and to have periodic trips back to corporate. While this was a helpful change, she noticed she still was spending far too much of her core work hours on the wedding. She next negotiated with her fiancé to help her with more of the wedding planning. With these small trial-and-error changes, gradually things improved. She began to be part of the core team again. Cindy is now happily married and has been promoted since the relocation.

These changes occur, as they did for Cindy, in what we see as a cycle of change (illustrated in Figure 7.1)—one that can be repeatedly followed as you experiment and use trial and error to move toward better ways of managing your life or to adapt to a new environment—like Cindy—as your life circumstances change. Cindy used several of the many tools for change we share in this chapter, including self-monitoring and reflection on whether her flexstyle was working for her, a readiness to change her flexstyle as she underwent a major life change, and a willingness to negotiate a new deal with coworkers and family members in an ongoing fashion. Whatever your flexstyle, you can use these same kinds of tools, along with many others we illustrate in this chapter, to help you move toward a better quality of life.

Change begins with self-awareness and assessment of the flexstyle you currently have and its benefits and pitfalls. For many people, just knowing in your head that you need to change won't be enough—you have to be motivated to change and take personal action. So, the next step after self-monitoring and awareness is to get over your natural reluctance to give up familiar ways of doing things, even if they aren't working for you anymore. From there, you must envision new ways of working and living, set the stage, and then actively experiment. From Captives to Fusion Lovers, everyone can use this process to refine or find a new flexstyle, using the tips and tools we provide throughout this chapter. Sometimes getting motivated to break out of old patterns and habits is the hardest step.

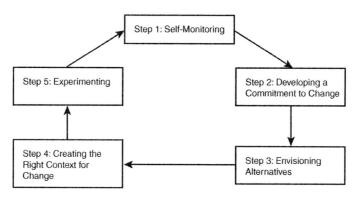

Figure 7.1 *A cycle of change for transforming flexstyles.*

The tools and approaches that we introduce in this chapter reflect three main lessons about change. First is that changing your flexstyle is something that requires not only thoughtful reflection, but it is also an ongoing process that needs your passion and commitment to succeed. Our second lesson is that, though change may seem daunting, you shouldn't go it alone. You can get guidance, ideas, and support from others, and you can also engage them in making changes that make sense not only for you but also for your partner, family, coworkers, or boss. Finally, making changes to your career and how it meshes with your personal life is often a messy start-and-stop-and-shift-directions kind of process, and the best way to make it through is to experiment with change and learn along the way. Often, as was the case for Cindy, you won't necessarily know what will work best in practice until you try it, and you may need to go through the change process a time or two before you settle into something that really works for you. So let's begin!

Step 1: Self-Monitoring

Researchers and consultants who help companies enact change have long recognized that the first step in any change process is for an awareness of the need for change to develop.[1] Organizations trying to evolve often begin with a type of self-assessment—an analysis of their strengths and weaknesses along with opportunities and challenges they face in their environment. Change at a personal level similarly needs to begin with some reflection. If you are reading this book and exploring the self-assessment exercises we presented in previous chapters, you are already engaged in this first step of change.

Another tool that you can use both at the beginning and after changing your flexstyle is something we call *habit tracking*. This involves self-monitoring of your behavior.[2] You can do this by keeping a time diary of when your moods are bad over the day, when you experience conflict or tension, and in what context. You can also reflect on how these feelings are linked to the kind of flexstyle you currently have, and this can help you understand how to craft change and identify trouble spots. It doesn't have to be something that takes a lot of time out of your already chaotic and crunched day. It can be as simple as keeping a chart, like the one shown in Table 7.1, on your computer or in a notebook on your nightstand and adding to it each day, for a week or two, until you can see patterns.

Table 7.1   *Habit Tracking*

Day	I felt overwhelmed, tense, or conflicted when...	Was I integrating or separating home and work or volleying between the two?	What were my options?	I felt most peaceful and happy when...
Monday	I realized the contractor was coming tomorrow afternoon at the same time I'd need to pick up my son from daycare and when I had a work deadline to meet.	Integrating: Reacting	Do it all myself, staying up late to finish the work. Negotiate with my spouse to meet with the contractor. Start to find new backups— maybe a new sitter—to help with daycare pickup. Negotiate to cut workload or get help from a colleague.	The house was quiet and I could focus to meet my work deadline. We all went out in the yard to work on the garden in the evening.

To learn the most from your own habit tracking records, watch for patterns. Do certain days or times always cause you stress? For example, maybe your Fridays are always too packed with activities, when you are always worn out, or perhaps that first hour after you return home and are transitioning from work to personal mode is consistently difficult. Think about the worst day that you wrote about. What made it unique? Were there any *triggers*——salient events that seemed to trigger the bad day? Read down the third column and check whether your tense moments tend to come when you are separating, blending, or volleying between the two. This can give you a signal of the direction in which you need to change. Push yourself to add one or two more options for solving conflicts that you had. You might initially believe you could only have dealt with the situation in the way you did, but try to come up with other possibilities. Think about the moments in your day that give you joy and about how you can create more of them.

CHANGE TIP #1
When habit tracking, identify moments of intense tension for you, as well as problem times and days that habitually cause you conflict. Note any triggers—events or situations that seem to accompany moments of tension.

CHANGE TIP #2
Reflect on recent situations where you have daily work-life conflicts, and develop two additional options for how you might have handled these conflicts in the future.

Habit tracking like this can be a useful beginning to improving how you mesh your work and personal life, as we've covered, but it is also a useful step to take as you embark on change. Set a goal for yourself about the kind of improvement you want to see in your life over time. Goals provide energy to sustain our efforts, and it's best to set goals that are specific, challenging, and measurable, rather than simply resolving something general like trying to "do your best."[3] Decide how dramatic a reduction in the number of conflicts you experience over a particular period of time you hope to achieve as you make changes to your flexstyle. Start small and then work up to bigger goals gradually. Then you can use habit tracking to review the outcomes of your personal change process and to identify setbacks or unintended outcomes that might necessitate a little fine-tuning.

CHANGE TIP #3
Set a goal for reducing the number of conflicts between work and home you experience and set a timeline for achieving that reduction. Use habit tracking periodically to check progress toward your goal.

Changing Your Flexstyle for Better Relationships
Between Work and Personal Life

In addition to habit tracking, the following questions can also provide helpful data as part of your self-assessment of the need to change your flexstyle:

1. To what extent is my current flexstyle draining time and energy away from what really matters to me?

2. Do the tradeoffs and stress that come with the flexstyle I'm currently using outweigh the benefits I am receiving?

3. Do my family, friends, or coworkers who are affected by my flexstyle think I need to make changes?

4. Can I envision more effective ways of managing my life that I would like to try?

5. Can I envision the barriers to change, and am I willing to surmount them?

6. Can I identify resources (money, people, knowledge, and so on) that may help me make a change?

7. Am I willing to consider both incremental changes to my current flexstyle as well as a major overhaul if necessary?

If you answered "yes" to several these questions, you are probably ready to commit to changing your flexstyle.

Step 2: Developing a Commitment to Change

Self-monitoring is a good start toward becoming CEO of your own life, but if you're like many other people, you might find your head filling with all kinds of reasons to stick with your current set of problems, even while you're carefully doing the assessments we provide. It's natural to feel reluctant to change. You might wonder about how things will go if you try to make a change. Will it be successful? Will it be such a difficult process that you'll find yourself wondering why you ever bothered? It can be difficult to risk the comfort that certainty brings—in this case, knowing what your days are going to be like, even if those days are chaotic and filled with more work and demands than you can ever juggle.

This resistance to change is natural but must be overcome if you want to take control of the flexibility in your life. An emotional commitment to change is essential. For many people we've spoken with, this commitment often develops in a key moment—or what we call a *critical incident*—when suddenly the person feels profoundly the limits of her current way of living. In the following sections, we share two stories that may seem minor to you but were actually vivid experiences for the people involved and turned out to be key tools in promoting change.

The Case of the Third-Grade Concert

Despite her busy career as a professional writer, Sally usually attended all of her third-grade son's school events held during the workday. But one afternoon, she had to miss a half-hour recorder concert in which her boy was playing. She had every intention of attending, but things at work got out of control at the last minute. Caught up in the work frenzy, Sally never made it to her son's concert. Though she rationalized that most of the other mothers did not work full time and thus found it easier to attend events, Sally deeply regretted the incident.

Sally could have used this incident to analyze her flexstyle and look for opportunities to change it for the better. If she had done so, she probably would have identified herself as a Reactor—an Integrator who feels little control over her life and who frequently experiences painful emotions such as guilt, regret, and frustration. Even though she had a flexible work schedule, she put in an average of 60 hours a week while also juggling care for her three young children. She was finding it increasingly difficult to attend school events during the workday. A relative novice in her job, she felt she had too much work to do in too little time. She also noticed that even when she attended school events, she had trouble enjoying them, because she was always worrying about work. Her spouse attended their children's concerts and other events when he could, but he had an even more stressful job than Sally did. His company had recently endured layoffs, so he and the other survivors had decided it was not a good time to miss work to fulfill family or personal needs.

Today, Sally's son is in high school. He still remembers the day his mother missed the recorder concert—and occasionally reminds her of it. If Sally had known ahead of time how important the concert was to him, she might have set her work aside and attended the performance. Her failure to attend had several causes. For one thing, Sally was having trouble managing her time and focusing on the right priorities at the right time—typical difficulties experienced by

Reactors. She also did not discuss ahead of time the possibility of missing the concert.

If Sally had talked earlier with her son about her work conflicts, she might have helped him understand why she couldn't attend his concert that one time. Equally valuable, she might have learned how important it was to him for her to go. In this case, she could have asked her husband (or perhaps a favorite aunt or grandparent) to attend the event so that at least one family member would be there.

Yet Sally had set up a historical family pattern in which she was the one who restructured her work life to meet family obligations. Had she negotiated with her husband or other family members to share participation in school events, planned her day better, or discussed things with her son ahead of time, she might have avoided this critical incident. The one silver lining of this experience is that it motivated Sally to change her flexstyle. It took years of gradual change to shift from being a Reactor to more of a Quality Timer, but Sally stuck with it, inspired by the conviction that she must never let something similar happen again.

Defining Moments: What Is Yours?

Some examples:

- When my wife threatened to walk out on me because I was always putting work ahead of our relationship
- When I realized the office was where I felt the most comfortable in life
- When I began to view uninterrupted work as a "religious experience"
- When my mother died before I had a chance to tell her I loved her
- When I realized I had no close friends
- When I kept looking at my Blackberry during my son's basketball game
- When I had a heart attack at 35

- When I chose to take a work call on my car cell phone and shushed my daughter when she was crying, instead of telling the person I would call him back
- When I felt so out of shape, I could no longer look at myself in the mirror
- When it became clear that the only thing that made me feel good about how I was handling my work and life was taking Prozac or drinking
- When my daughter said to me, "Mom, I feel like you're with me, but you're really not with me."

The Case of the Family Chauffeur

Bob had a vision: He would be a different kind of man than his father had been—a much more involved and dedicated family man. His father, a workaholic, had been only a faint presence during Bob's childhood. To achieve his vision of being a better parent, Bob had established certain systems. For example, since his spouse had a less flexible job than his, he agreed to drive his son to all of his weekly sports practices and out-of-town competitions. But because Bob had an extremely demanding job, he tried to fulfill all his professional responsibilities by working intensely at the office—often discovering that he didn't have time to get all his tasks done.

Bob was also committed to being a better son and to helping his elderly mother. In her 80s, Bob's mom needed help with all manner of small activities of daily life. Bob helped her interpret her bills if they changed format and she couldn't figure them out, made phone calls for her because she couldn't understand automated call menus and didn't know how to use a computer to go online, made sure her stove was working when she thought it wasn't, and performed minor repairs in her home. The hardest task to juggle was driving his mom to her various doctor appointments. He knew it meant a lot to her, but he found it hard to take even more time out his day to shepherd her to her eye doctor to follow up on her cataract surgery and to other appointments. As she got older, Bob found there were more and more of these issues to take care of.

As a consequence of his flexstyle, Bob occasionally had to miss meetings with colleagues or clients, and he worried that these incidents hurt his professional standing. He wondered sometimes whether he was sacrificing too much work in his efforts to show his commitment to his family, especially when he would run into a colleague who had started at the same level as Bob but who had been promoted well beyond him.

Things might have continued in this way had Bob not experienced what for him was a critical incident. One week, his son's practice ran late, forcing Bob to not only miss an important company social hour, but also have to reschedule a doctor appointment for his aging mom. He went overboard losing his temper with his son, and Bob recognized that the stress of living this way was too much for him. Things would have to change. Bob decided he would sit down with his family, discuss his predicament, and work together with them to figure out some new ways of doing things.

Making Use of Regret

Bob should prepare for the discussion with his family and not just "wing it." He should think first about what his priorities and preferences are. How much work is he willing to sacrifice to his family? What family needs are a higher priority? Is it worth it to miss work to take his mother to an appointment with her neurologist but not to her family physician for a simple checkup? Could he miss the occasional practice for his son if he made it to all the key games? Just being more conscious about these tradeoffs could help Bob, because at least he would feel that any career advancement he sacrificed was by choice and not because he was trapped in a bad pattern. Bob should also anticipate his family members' reactions and think about how he could respond to any concerns they might have. His mom, for example, might be uncomfortable with a service driving her to her appointments but might feel better if she got to interview drivers and help select one. Engaging the whole family in brainstorming solutions (and following other tips we cover later in Chapter 9, "Negotiating a New Flexstyle and a Life that Works on Your Terms") would go a long way to solving Bob's problems. And, rather than simply feeling badly about yelling at his son, Bob will have used the motivation this event provided to help him take control and better mesh his work and personal life.

The stories of Sally and Bob illustrate how a critical moment can provide the emotional catalyst for change. Try to identify critical incidents in your own life. Ask yourself whether there have been any times lately when you wished you had managed the blending of your work and home differently. Pay attention to regret. It provides a signpost pointing you toward moments where your values have not been in line with your behaviors, and also points you toward changes you'll be committed to following through. Reminding yourself of the regret you've experienced in a key moment can help to sustain your energy and commitment to change.

CHANGE TIP #4
Identify moments in your life where you have a lingering regret about how you juggled work and personal life. This regret can provide emotional commitment to change.

Step 3: Envisioning Alternatives

Real vision cannot be understood in isolation from the idea of purpose. By purpose, I mean an individual's sense of why he is alive.

Peter Senge, change guru and author of The Fifth Discipline[4]

Spend some time imagining what your ideal work and home situations would be. What would a perfect evening for you be like? Would you be home with family, gathered on the sofa sharing a movie and popcorn? Or out for dinner with a work colleague, brainstorming on a new project? Do you see yourself interrupting either scenario? Does e-mail on the beach during your vacation sound normal or horrifying to you? Answers to these kinds of questions can help you to identify what you really care about and the direction in which you should start moving to be more in control of your life.

To think through the range of options you have for controlling flexibility and meshing your home and work life, it can also help to keep an eye out for role models. You'll find many as you read through this book and the stories of individuals we've met. But you'll also find others in your own life. Pay attention to how your coworkers manage their flexstyle, and you might be surprised to find different ways of doing things, even in the same organization.

CHANGE TIP #5
Imagine your ideal flexstyle and look for role models.

While you're thinking about how you can change your flexibility working type, also consider how you can reduce the level of demands on yourself. Don't forget to manage the workload: Customize your job or family life by cutting back 10%, so you can focus on what is more meaningful to you, what you do best, and what you enjoy. Just cutting back 10% to 20% on the tasks you least enjoy will lead to many other positive effects.

Consider the case of Mike, a general manager in retail. He had been a Reactor and now tries to be a Quality Timer. He varies how he works each day, eats better, and takes vacations more regularly than he ever did before. He also negotiated changes with his boss—some tactics that we discuss in greater depth in Chapter 9.

What Mike Did to Make Change

Mike is a general manager at a major home improvement firm. For years he had been a Reactor. He is 40 years old and 60 pounds overweight with a wife who works at a bank and two kids. His dad died early from a heart attack. Five years ago he went on medication because he found out he was developing high blood pressure just like his dad. He also found out he suffers from a disease that affects his ability to sleep well.

He now tries to live each day differently:

1. He gets up early and focuses on the job tasks requiring the highest quality thinking from 6:00 a.m. to 7:30 a.m. He finds that he gets as much done in that hour and a half as he gets done in three hours in the afternoon. He runs errands in the afternoon and now regularly stops working at 5:00 p.m.

2. He talked to his boss about the need to reduce his stress, by enabling him to have more control over workload and by making sure the best subordinates are assigned to projects he works on.

3. He also works hard to turn off work more, whereas in the past he used to fixate on work all the time. Now he religiously takes a week vacation every six months. Most recently he went out of the country to Jamaica.

---

4   He makes a point to eat better. He used to each only high choles-
terol food. Now he tries to eat mostly salads at lunch and also
tries to not buy junk food. He takes the time to cook and eat
home-cooked meals with his family.

5.   He chooses to work on jobs that give him the most income to
free up time for the rest of his life. Mike commented, "My job is
10 hours a day but the other 14 is my life."

CHANGE TIP #6
Manage your workload.

You can also think at the team or group level and create substitutes. The
media would have us think of work-family conflict as an individual problem, but
it is a collective issue that requires not only individual change but also a change
in our life social system—our family group and our work group. If we are in a
family structure or a work structure that constrains our control and choice over
how we make use of flexibility, this will create problems and conflicts no matter
how hard we try to do it all. We need to develop backup systems in our lives so
that we are not the only go-to person and so that we can focus on our priorities
and key values. If it's critical to you that you always be available to meet key work
deadlines, you might need backup at home—whether it is a backup babysitter or
a friend, spouse, or family member who can provide sick care backup. Similarly
at work, it can help to have cross-training so that the boss or customer has someone else to go to.

CHANGE TIP#7
Create substitutes for your own efforts to allow you to focus on key
priorities.

Step 4: Creating the Right Context for Change

Discuss and share the good things that happen to you with others who matter to
you in both domains—work and home. This will help you learn about the benefits of *interpersonal capitalization boosters.*[5] This is the idea that simply the act

of sharing with others, such as your spouse, the news of a positive event increases its effects on you to an even greater extent. When sharing about something, you get an additional event that is a boost beyond the event itself. For example, when you share a positive experience that happened at work with your spouse at home, this will make you even happier at home—you get a boost. The same is true at work. Do this both at work and at home to cross domains.

CHANGE TIP #8
Share positive events that happen at work or home with others to get the added benefit of an interpersonal capitalization boost.

You can also seek emotional support from others. Finding others in similar situations and with shared concerns over work and home is something you can do and something both you and the others in the support network benefit from. It does not have the same potential to require adjustment or sacrifice on the other individuals' parts and does not require the more complex processes we turn to in Chapters 9 and 10, "Not Going It Alone: Making Sustainable Change at Your Workplace."

Consider Cindy, who we introduced in our opening to this chapter. After she began working out of the satellite office, things changed for the better. She thought that being in a more traditional work setting would be helpful to her in terms of returning to a focus on work, even though there were no people in the office in her same job or department. But the biggest benefit of her new work arrangement turned out to be that a handful of other workers there were also working in long-distance arrangements. A couple of them had even gone through a similar process, and they laughed together over the struggles they all had integrating because it wasn't what they wanted, and they hadn't been able to figure out how to be work-first Separators at home. Cindy found that having others in a similar work arrangement to talk with was also helpful when occasional glitches came up—like when they had to participate in conference calls with others at a different time zone, and this meant taking the call at home.

CHANGE TIP #9
Find others you can relate to for encouragement and brainstorming how to deal with shared challenges.

Step 5: Experimentation

---

*The only way to make sense out of change is to plunge into it,
move with it, and join the dance!*

Alan Watts[6]

If you're thinking of changing your flexstyle, or adopting a new one, you won't truly know what will work best until you experiment a little. Herminia Ibarra, INSEAD Business School professor and author of *Working Identity: Unconventional Strategies for Reinventing Your Career* emphasizes how important it is to become engaged in change and to look at it as a sometimes long and often iterative process. She says: "We discover the true possibilities by doing—trying out new activities, reaching out to new groups, finding new role models, and reworking our story as we tell it to those around us. What we want clarifies with experience and validation from others along the way."

We agree and think that individuals often have the most success in changing their flexstyle when they start with small experiments. This can mean taking one separation or integration tactic, for example, and trying it out. It could be something as simple as hiring some child-care help during a stressful time to reduce the demands on yourself, as Derek did in the following example. Over time, you can discover which particular way of living out your flexstyle works best for you.

Craig's List to the Rescue

Derek and his wife both focused on busy jobs during the day and were finding the "witching hour"—when they arrived home from work and tried to transition to family time—impossible. It was a "switch from all work to all family...not all [the] fun stuff of family, but the unfun stuff—whiny kids, cooking dinner, dishes piled high." The solution? Advertising on Craig's List for some help at a critical time. They were successful in finding a former nurse who, for $15 per hour, comes to their home a few nights a week to ease the burden and provide a buffer time. "We bought ourselves some extra time, so we could rearrange life to focus on the rewarding aspects of being a parent and a spouse."

Remember that small changes can especially go a long way when you are a leader in your organization. Take the example of Roger, a partner in a large consulting firm. He was concerned that his staff were working hours well in excess of what was going to work well in the long run, either for the people or the organization. And he wanted people to stop using flexibility to simply overwork. Rather than just making a policy to limit work hours, he also started to make a "point of not checking or leaving voicemail on weekends or during vacations," and to lead by example.[7] We'll return to these issues of organizational leadership in Chapter 10.

CHANGE TIP #10
Experiment with small changes.

Conclusion

Opportunities abound for you to make changes to your flexstyle. Anyone can use the process we describe in this chapter to work toward a better quality of life and meshing of work and personal life. Articulating your identity—who you are and who you want to be—can help you decide which changes can benefit you and those around you most. Experimenting with even small alterations in how you manage your many commitments can then help you refine your approach and find a way of living out a flexstyle that works best for you. For those who desire only a small improvement in their strategy for managing flexibility, these small changes may be sufficient. But for others, particularly Captives, Job Warriors, and Reactors, who may want to fundamentally shift the way they juggle work and home, small changes may be used in combination. Even if a big change is needed, sometimes taking a first small step is the easiest way to begin.

In Chapter 8, "Tailoring Change to Your Particular Flexstyle," we move beyond the general change process and tools outlined here to some suggestions specific to different flexstyles. We devote Chapter 9 to negotiation, a tactic for change that is so critical that it deserves more of our attention. Finally, in Chapter 10 we explore more of how change for you might be related to your work group or organizational context and how you can be a leader for positive change to support not only your own flexstyle but also those of others.

Top 12 Strategies Everyone Can Use to Gain Flexstyle Control

- Try Habit Tracking.
- Challenge Self to Consider More Flexstyle Options.
- Establish Goals and Timetables To Reduce Daily Conflicts.
- Use Defining Moments As Change Catalyst.
- Draw on Regret to Avoid Repeating Mistakes.
- Find Role Models.
- Imagine Your Ideal.
- Create Substitutes.
- Reduce Workload.
- Share positive events to get an added boost.
- Find Others To Create Social Support Systems
- Experiment With Small Changes.

chapter eight

Tailoring Change to Your Particular Flexstyle

Currently, I don't subscribe to the workday idea. I get what I need to get done for home and for work. Some days home takes longer; most days work takes longer. Particularly, now that my wife is sick, I think it's fair that if I am willing to give more than a 10-hour day to the company, people I work with need to understand there are times when I need to take care of personal things as well during normal business hours. I hate talking about my family situation with people at work, but things really are stressful and not working out very well since I am always managing last minute conflicts.

Jon, professional, married with two children under five and a partner with a debilitating disease

Gaining Control, Countering Tradeoffs, and Exploring Flexstyle Options

Jon had always been a career-driven Work Firster, and that focus continued even after he and his wife, Vanessa, had their two children. They hadn't planned to have a traditional way of splitting household tasks, but somehow that evolved over time. His wife found that she enjoyed being home with the kids more than she anticipated, and so delayed going back to work after their daughter was born. Then baby #2 arrived quickly, and it seemed to make little sense for both young children to be in daycare, and it was just easier for everyone if Vanessa managed the household and children, while Jon focused on work. All that changed when Vanessa was diagnosed with multiple sclerosis and had an acute episode that left her incapacitated for months. Overnight, Jon became a Reactor, responsible not only for work, but also for everything including care for his wife, the household, and their kids. Jon hopes that eventually his wife's health will improve, and that things will get back to normal (or something closer to it). But in the meantime, he feels like he is drowning and not keeping up either at home or at work, and something has to change.

You may be like Jon or know someone like him. Jon needs to drastically alter his current flexstyle and try out new strategies for change that are particular to a major, new life direction he must take. He is facing new challenges in his private life, and his old way of working, where he was able to shut himself off from family for 10 to 12 hours, is creating problems since he doesn't know how to adapt to more flexible relationships between work and personal life. He needs to do much more in the family arena now that his wife is sick, but he and his employer have not adapted to a new way of working.

In this chapter we take a step beyond the general change process and tips provided in Chapter 7, "Changes Everyone Can Make to Improve Quality of Life." We offer suggestions for how you can make changes specific to a particular flexstyle or situation. There are three main approaches for making changes specific to a flexstyle: gain greater control over work-life relationships, minimize tradeoffs, and explore new flexstyle options (see Figure 8-1). For each approach, we consider Jon's situation and give examples of how to apply the strategy to make things work better for him and other Reactors. We then also give tips on how to apply the change approach to people using other flexstyles who may want to make changes.

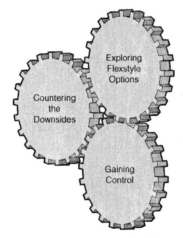

Figure 8-1 *Specific change strategies.*

Change Strategy 1: Gaining Control

The first type of change strategies are geared toward giving individuals more control over how they manage work and personal life relationships. These are aimed at helping individuals whose flexstyles make them feel unhappy and lacking control. Typically, Reactors, Job Warriors, and Captives all feel they lack control, their work and personal lives are at odds, and they want to make fundamental change.

If you're a Reactor like Jon, you likely feel that the key thing you lack control over is the number of demands you face and when they occur. Work e-mails, pages, and calls come in while you're trying to wrestle with the needs of your family, and it's all just a bit much. The solution for you might be to become a Fusion Lover, Quality Timer, or Work or Family First Separator, but whichever you chose, you'll need to start to gain control over the demands on you. People who are in control feel they face a manageable level of job and family pressures and have more predictability in the demands they face. They also have the ability to say "yes," "no," or "not now, but later," instead of being tugged this way and that at the whim of others. For ideas on how you might create those conditions in your life, read the rest of Jon's story.

Application: How Gaining Control Could Help a Reactor Like Jon

To regain control, Jon needs both to reduce the overall level of combined work and family demands on himself and work to gradually shift from reacting back to his preferred style of being a Work-First Separator or at least a Quality Timer.

Making Others Aware of New Life Demands and Get Agreement to Support New Needs. At work, unless Jon is self-employed and can afford to simply cut back on his clients temporarily, he will likely have to get the agreement of others in his organization before scaling back his work. In the short term, he might need to take advantage of a personal leave policy at his work to devote time to getting systems set up to manage his wife's illness and its impacts on his family. Longer term, he might even want to consider a reduced-load work arrangement, in which he would work fewer hours, for a period of time. Or, if he works on a team, his colleagues might agree to cover for him for awhile, on the understanding that he'll make it up later. Making these kinds of arrangements should be easy for Jon because he has a good reputation in the company for being a solid worker but still may require some negotiation—give and take and persuasion. And for that he could consider the sort of detailed advice on negotiation tools and strategies that will be shared in Chapter 9, "Negotiating a New Flexstyle and a Life That Works on Your Terms." Jon also could think about how to lessen the demands on him at home by seeking out some help. He knows, for example, that many of their friends and family would be happy to come by from time to time with a meal, and even that small thing could be a big help. He just needs to not be too proud to accept their help.

Set Access Rules. Along with getting the demands he faces down to a level he can cope with, Jon needs to be strategic when faced with a demand from work or home. Whereas previously he might have checked e-mail and happily accepted phone calls from colleagues 24/7, in his current situation he might need to set limits on both this and family interruptions. He needs to think about establishing something we call *access rules*—guidelines for others for when and how they can contact you. E-mail might be less intrusive than a page, if Jon could give himself only set times to deal with e-mail, for example.

Don't Wait to Ask for Extra Help and Resources to Handle Increased Demands. Jon may also consider hiring a nanny or homecare nurse to help with family demands or ask his boss to give him someone to help with his work demands during this period as he sorts out his values, needs, and new preferred life bucket allocation.

Limit Multitasking and Try Taking Mini-Breaks. Although in the long term, Jon may think about shifting back to being a Work-First Separator, in the short term when he has to meld a lot of his personal and work responsibilities, he can limit multitasking and the number of times he is actively doing both work and family tasks in the same time and space. Sometimes just taking a break and having a period of separation can be helpful for someone like Jon; for example, if he finds himself working from home temporarily so he can better connect with the home health-care aide assisting his wife and be there for emergencies the nanny can't handle with the kids. He may also want to set aside a couple hours from time to time when he can exclusively focus on one or the other to help with the mental and emotional strain of integrating when he doesn't want to. A couple hours when the grandparents are covering at home and Jon gets to go to the office could help him feel more in control of his life.

The tips discussed in the preceding paragraphs apply to most Reactors. But what if you are a Job Warrior or Captive? The following sections offer some tips for each of those specific styles related to gaining control.

Control Strategies for Job Warriors

TIP #1
Create substitutes to enable you to control the timing of separation.

If you are a Job Warrior you have some things in common with Jon. For you as well, one issue is the overall workload you face, and negotiation at home and at work can be one important solution to that. The other main challenge you may struggle with as a Job Warrior is getting control of *when* you separate and when you instead more fluidly meld your work and personal life. Most often, Job Warriors separate during periods of intense work and while traveling, and then feel compelled to integrate after they are home to deal with the personal needs that have accumulated while they've been focused on work. If you are in this pattern and it doesn't fit with your needs and values, you can consciously try to gain control of the time when you mesh work and family. For example, if you must attend a conference each year in August that forces you to be away the week of your youngest child's birthday, you might ask your colleague on the project to cover your presentation every other year so that you don't always miss your child's birthday.

TIP #2
Create portable virtual integration tactics.

If you want to have more control and ability to be involved in family life even when you are traveling or working long hours on a major project at the office, you may create times that your family can contact you. For example, you could have your child e-mail you his homework if you need to help with that, or call your dad's doctor to speak with her about the cancer surgery. You could also keep your cell phone on and invite your family and friends to call anytime after 5:00 p.m. so that even though you are in another city and could work all evening, this would make you take a break and speak with your family.

Small changes like these can help you to feel more involved at home even while you're on the road. And the reason for connecting could be that you want to be more emotionally involved each day. Dave, for example, found he had to travel more and more from the satellite office he worked at to headquarters. He didn't mind this, except that his children were at an age where they were missing him at bedtime. Dave made a promise—before leaving on his next work trip—that he would always call to say goodnight and even to read a bedtime story. On the trip, Dave kept his promise, even though with time differences it was sometimes tough. Dave also occasionally had to miss out on a fun dinner with his colleagues or on a bit of downtime in the hotel. But it was worth it. It meant a lot to Dave and his kids to keep this bit of continuity in the nightly routine and made it easier in the end for Dave to face the next trip.

TIP #3
Create workable transitions.

Or you might be a Job Warrior who wants to separate more, even during times that you are at home or your workload is more manageable. Perhaps you find it hard to shift into full-on family mode the minute you walk through the door after a long and grueling trip away. You need some time to decompress. Over time you might want to become more of a Work or Family Firster, but for now you can start thinking about how you could incorporate a bit more separation into your routine. Using travel times to transition from work mode to family mode can be helpful, as noted previously. Beyond that, if it's tough for you to do both work and family during periods, consider sequencing them. That is, if you have two days at home after three days of travel, rather than having both of them a blur of doing a little bit of everything, see whether you can devote a day and a half to work and take a dedicated half day for home. This could require some discussion with both your family and your boss. Before you have this conversation, think about their expectations and whether another arrangement might suit you better and still allow you to meet your responsibilities in both realms. This kind of tactic could be useful not only for your family but also for your own personal health and well-being. For example, Professor Mina Westman has found that coming home after a business trip can be very demanding stresswise and experienced differently for men and women. Her study found, for example, that compared to their male counterparts, female managers with families at home to care for, have significantly lower stress levels while traveling and significantly higher stress levels when they return home to re-enter and handle all of the domestic matters that often pile up while they are on the road.[1]

Control Strategies for Captives

TIP #4
Negotiate for flexible work options and try out a new flexstyle.

If you're a Captive, the control issue that you likely wrestle with the most is that you are stuck in an inflexible job, and you often can't choose when you can respond to a personal need. Most Captives have no choice but to focus on work at work, and their personal and family needs suffer. For years, consultants and academics who study work-family relationships have been advocating flexible work arrangements as a solution to this particular problem. As we've shown, flexibility without control has as many problems as being a Captive. So, you may want to negotiate with your supervisor for more flexible policies—flexible hours, family-related leave, telecommuting options, and so on. But if you do so, be sure that you are conscious about choosing the flexstyle you will adopt and don't inadvertently become a Reactor. Asking for this kind of change in the company for which you work can be most effectively done if you are not just looking for an individual arrangement, but if instead you can be part of changing work in ways that also change the culture of your company and benefit your coworkers. Then, it's not just about you getting a special deal—which your coworkers may resent. As long as the change is compatible with getting work done, it may also be better for the organization as a whole. For more on leading change in your organization, keep reading on to Chapter 10, "Not Going It Alone: Making Sustainable Change at Your Workplace." Table 8.1 summarizes some of the strategies for gaining control.[1]

Table 8.1 *Strategies for Gaining Control*

Flexstyle	Main Control Issue	Fixes
Reactor	Not enough control over the timing and amount of both work and family demands	Negotiate to reduce the level of demands on you, from work or home.
		Look for resources—family, friends, community—that can help you to meet the demands that you've struggled with on your own before.
		Prioritize and then negotiate access rules for when colleagues and family can get in touch or interrupt to limit the number of times you must switch between work and family and give you more control over it.

Flexstyle	Main Control Issue	Fixes
Reactor (cont.)		Limit multitasking and try to build small separation "breaks" into your day or week if you want to move toward volleying or separating, rather than becoming a Fusion Lover.
		Minimize the number of different things you are responsible for at any given time to reduce switching costs.
		Consider leaving a job situation where there is no potential of gaining flexibility and the ability to control that flexibility, so you can have a life that works for you.
		Make others aware of life demands and your needs.
Job Warrior	Not enough control over workload and over when you must switch from integrating to separating	Create substitutes to enable you to control the timing of when you must separate.
		Negotiate for reduced workload, less travel, or assistance at work and home for part of year.
		Create portable virtual integration tactics.
		Create workable transitions.
		Don't assume you have to integrate at home and separate while on the road or in a heavy work phase.
Captive	Not enough schedule control over whether and when you can respond to personal or family needs at work	Negotiate a more flexible work arrangement, but be sure it's one where you are in control of the flexibility.
		Consider an organizationwide solution where flexible work and other family-friendly policies are made available to all your peers as well.

Change Strategy 2: Reducing the Disadvantages of Your Current Flexstyle

The second main type of change strategy is to try out new behaviors that directly tackle and minimize the downsides of your current flexstyle. Take Jon as an example. In the short run, he probably has to keep the flexstyle he currently has. He may have no choice but to highly integrate until his wife is better, but he can try to fine-tune and minimize the downsides or tradeoffs of his particular style. He cannot totally go back to being a Work Firster in the short run, but he can try to minimize the drawbacks of integrating.

Application: How Countering the Downsides Could Help Someone Like Jon

Jon can try to consciously reduce the negative effects of integrating. He can guard against the feeling that he has to be a "hero" and take on everything his wife used to do and more. He also needs to learn to sometimes say "no" and not take on too much. He also must learn to trust others for many things, but especially caregiving, something he didn't have to previously do with a dedicated, full-time family caregiver. So, although his wife had been home with the kids, Jon might need to sort out at least a temporary (but high-quality) daycare arrangement and then, rather than calling repeatedly to check on the children, trust the child-care providers to call him in an emergency. Something small like this can help to reduce the number of times Jon must switch to focus on home matters while at work and help cut down on his feelings of being overwhelmed and exhausted with juggling it all.

Jon also needs to minimize switching costs from work demands. Except in an emergency, he should try not to check his e-mail in the evenings and on weekends so that he can focus on family then. Or if he has a heavy work-load, he can stay late one night so that he can focus and get it all done and then be able to focus on family when at home. He also needs to avoid mul-titasking. For example, if someone calls him at work from home, and he is in a meeting, rather than taking the call then, he can ask, "Is this an emer-gency?" And if not, he can then say, "Can I call you back?" The same goes for receiving work calls at home. Jon should try to take them only when he is not multitasking and should screen his calls and then call people back when he can focus on work.

Table 8.2 lists the flexstyles described in this book, their associated major tradeoffs, and suggestions for mitigating the stress resulting from the tradeoffs. For example, if you are unhappy with the outcomes of being a Family Firster, and yet don't want to shift to another style, you might work to reduce the negative career threats from being sometimes out of touch with work. Some research by Professor Zoe Barsness and others has shown that remote workers, who share these kinds of worries, often are successful in improving their performance if they increase their efforts to manage supervisors' impressions of them, and you may also try this.[2] Of course, not all the downsides of each flexstyle can be easily overcome without considering a major life change to a new flexstyle, particularly if you're a Captive, Reactor, or Job Warrior. More drastic changes or a shift in style will be necessary in some cases, and we turn to those solutions in the next section.

Table 8.2 *Simple Fixes for Flexstyle Downsides*

Flexstyle	Primary Disadvantages	Tips for Better Managing Your Flexstyle
Family Firster	Negative impact on career Possible negative coworker, client, or supervisor reactions Lack of support across work and family domains	Contribute unique value at work in ways that don't impinge on family time. For example, volunteer to take on a task that your colleagues aren't interested in. Build a reputation for credibility and reliability at work. For instance, make your regular work hours well known to others and stick to them. And cultivate positive relationships with your boss and coworkers by helping others in need and providing positive feedback to others.
Work Firstar	Risk of missing out on key family events or personal interests Potential for overwork and burnout Lack of support across work and family domains	Carve out quality time for family or self—for example, by taking an afternoon off occasionally. Use your time and energy wisely: Work on the most important projects during the time of day when you have the most energy. Designate certain times of day for checking and responding to e-mail (rather than responding each time your monitor chimes). Make lunch appointments to force yourself to take a midday break. Keep a weekly log documenting the amount of time you spend on work versus nonwork priorities. If you find that you typically leave little or no time for nonwork interests, take steps to improve the balance.
Captive	Miss key family and life events Role conflict and stress Less developed nonwork life Families/friends can become short-changed or victims of our nonwork demands Lack of cross-domain support	Find a stress-management approach that works for you. Simple techniques such as regular exercise can reduce stress and the health problems associated with it.[3] Use your entire work break for personal revitalization.

S E P A R A T O R S

Table 8.2 *(continued)*

Flexstyle	Primary Disadvantages	Tips for Better Managing Your Flexstyle
Quality Timer	Confusion over which demand is more pressing; risk of pursuing both work and network activities in middle-of-the-road way, with mediocre outcomes for both Role confusion possible for family and coworkers Job creep Increased cognitive complexity Difficulty setting priorities Role confusion	Block out large chunks of time for focusing on work or family/personal/community life—you'll reduce switching costs and give your best attention to each role. Have periods where you turn off communication devices such as cell phone and Blackberry.
Job Warrior	Difficulty switching from separating and a focusing on work while traveling to integrating with family when home Fatigue Overloaded weekends spent on mundane household tasks that workers with more flexible schedules can do in the week Miss life and work events happening during the week Vulnerable to breakdown of support system; may not work for someone who lacks a partner who can pitch hit while you are on the road or in a heavy work phase Sunday night blues as leaving for road or another grinding long work week Job creep Increased cognitive complexity Difficulty setting priorities Role confusion	Use travel time to ease transition. Begin shifting modes while in transit to ease adjustment after you arrive. For example, stop thinking about work on the drive home and start thinking about weekend activities.[4] Focus your time on activities you most value when you are home.

VOLLEYERS

INTEGRATORS

Flexstyle	Primary Disadvantages	Tips for Better Managing Your Flexstyle
Fusion Lover	Job or family creep (long days) Others' escalating expectations about your availability Switching costs from frequent transitions Seen as unprofessional if integrate family or other personal interests into work	Track your work hours for a week or two, along with the number and length of "breaks" you take. You'll become more conscious of destructive work patterns. Limit the number of breaks per day. Set dates for revisiting whether your flexstyle approach is working for you.
Reactor	Others' escalating expectations that you'll be available whenever they need you Switching costs from frequent transitions between work and non-work—higher even than other Integrators because dislike switching Job or family creep (long days) Seen as unprofessional if integrate family into work time Overload and loss of feeling of control Frustration and burnout Dissatisfaction with performance in both work and personal life roles	Resist the urge to take on more and more, at work or at home. Develop realistic expectations of yourself and communicate them to others. Try to minimize the number of times you switch between work and non-work.

Change Strategy 3: Exploring New Flexstyles

Sometimes tactics to gain control or tinkering with your current style to minimize its downsides are not sufficient to improve your life. The third major change individuals can make is to explore new flexstyle options that you believe might work better. You might try out one of the tactics for a few weeks and follow habit tracking to see whether it is leading to positive results for you at work and home.

Let's return to Jon, who you met at the beginning of this chapter. While his wife is ill, and he has to juggle greater family involvement with ongoing work obligations, he feels he has to integrate more than he would like. But while this is not ideal for him, he can at least experiment with different ways of integrating to explore whether some might be more positive for him and his family. And longer term, he can separate more and shift to being a Quality Timer or Work Firster again.

Application: How Exploring Flexstyle Options Could Help Someone Like Jon

A reluctant Reactor like Jon could apply the flexstyle options listed in Table 8-3 for integrating to allow him to not just react to work and family all at once. He should try out positive aspects of Fusion Loving and Quality Timing to develop new ways of working that better suit his preferences. After all, just because he now has to integrate work and family more until his wife gets better doesn't mean he has to integrate blindly in every way. For example, Jon could ask himself which types of integration would most help his family and yet allow him to still focus on work when he can. He could plan to be physically available for family when needed (but perhaps less so to friends, given the level of family demands he faces now) and keep his cell phone on for emergencies at work. But he might try to encourage mental separation more during the workday to enhance quality working time. He could purposefully choose not to talk about work and family, or to keep pictures of family on his desk at work. For him, avoiding as much mental integration as possible while at work might help him to get work done in less time and to feel less overwhelmed. While he is at work, he would spend his precious time trying to be as productive as possible and would let people know his work hours to maximize his work time, handling

---

matters that require face-to-face contact. The same when he is at home. He should try to mentally turn off work and focus on his kids and wife. He may need to develop transition tactics that enable him to separate, such as listening to the radio on the long ride home or going out to walk the dog when he first gets to the door.

In the rest of this chapter, we give tips and tools specific to making change to use each of the three main flexstyle types more effectively. If you are going to try one of these types, you could take several of these tips as a way to experiment.

Exploring Flexstyle Options: Tactics for Integrating Work and Personal Life More Effectively

TIP #5
Take actions to be more available to family, friends, and coworkers at meaningful or critical life periods.

If you are one who has traditionally not been available to your work or family at critical times, one action you can take is to change the access rules and try to be more available during these periods.

Take Dave, a Job Warrior who is trying to be more of a Fusion Lover. He works as a program client executive and travels extensively. Dave says that over time he has tried to "integrate work and family more because they are not two separate pieces of his life." Indeed, integrating "humanizes his work." As part of his effort to blend the many dimensions of his life, Dave allows family members to contact him any time he is in his home office or on the road. He also helps take care of his mother-in-law, who lives with Dave and his wife. Though she doesn't require physical assistance, she no longer drives. Moreover, she does not communicate effectively. Thus, she occasionally needs help with tasks such as phoning in prescriptions or making doctor appointments. Though Dave's wife cares for her mother every day, he also assists as needed.

To make a strategy such as Dave's work, you probably must be an above-average performer at work who is able to get work done when not attending to family. It takes a lot of discipline to make this strategy work.

The same is true at home. If there is a critical assignment at work and you are supposed to be on vacation that day, you could let your boss know to call you if it is really imperative. You would need to let your family know you are doing this because if you didn't you wouldn't have been able to go on the vacation. This would then minimize dissatisfaction with your integrating at this key work period.

Application: How Even Captives Can Make Personal Choices to Gain Flexibility

Andrew, a single male, works at Manufacturing Inc., a plant that has an overtime culture with people working 60-70 hours per week. At first glance, it seems as though Andrew is a Captive with little personal life outside his work day. However, this is not the case with Andrew.

Andrew is able to return home during his lunch hour to let his dog out, play with his dog, and eat a well-balanced meal. How does he do this? He chooses to live 5 minutes away from the plant and by having a short commute, he is able to create time for a personal life and to be more available to family—even the family dog. By examining Andrew's life, we can see that, even when it appears there is no hope to integrate and make a life, simple choices such as living close to work can create flexibility in a seemingly inflexible situation.

TIP #6
Set personal ground rules to help yourself focus on the priority of the moment and be willing to restructure to finish tasks that are critical to keep deadlines.

People who want to integrate more can do so by focusing on what seems to have priority at the moment. Your assessment of what constitutes a priority depends on the situation: Different demands will seem more or less critical at different times. Neena, for example, explains that "if something comes up with the kids, then that is the priority." This is because she is a Fusion Lover who is tilting toward family first. When family or personal demands encroach on Neena's work, she gets up early or stays up late to make up the time. Integrating helps her focus on what is most important to her at every moment, and she will gladly "sacrifice sleep or my lunch hour to do that."

TIP #7
Briefly talk about work and family at the office and at home...within limits to allow for empathy, and cross-domain understanding.

The Integrators we've met tend not to draw lines between when they talked about work with their family or vice versa. Instead, they share some information across both realms. Ben, for instance, says that the key to integrating (for him) is to convey information across both domains, but not so much that either domain dominates the other. In his words:

You just want to make sure that you have enough quality of life where you're spending time with family, and you're not spending all the time talking about work challenges. Share for 10 to 15 minutes; then get out of it and on to your personal life....Too much conversation leads to domination, [which is] not a good family dynamic. Same with business. Sometimes you can bring [family] up and make things more humanistic [at work], but if you bring it up too much, you're not going to get anywhere...but it does warm up conversation.

TIP #8
Establish new rituals and routines.

Small new rituals and routines can help you step up your efforts to integrate. For example, suppose you have an inflexible job in an office that affords few opportunities to interact with family or friends, yet you see yourself as a good partner, parent, and sibling, as well as a worthy friend. You don't want to put those relationships at risk by letting work cut you off from these individuals. In this case, you can still integrate more. To illustrate, set up a weekly or monthly lunch date with a valued friend or your spouse. Or even if you work long hours, commit to having dinner at home with the family, even if you have to return to the office afterward.

Of course, if you're a Captive, these small changes may not be enough to help you to take control of your life. In this situation, you might want to consider the larger-scale changes we introduce in Chapters 9 and 10. Still, rituals like those just described can help you articulate what you care most about and demonstrate to others your commitment to nurturing those priorities.

Table 8.3 shows the tips we have developed through our interviews for integrating when you are at the office or at home.

Table 8.3 *Tactics for Integrating More Effectively*

	Integrating in the Office	Integrating at Home
Physical integration	Work close to home so you can easily run home at lunch or handle a small errand and return to the office. Move closer to work if you currently have a long or difficult commute.	Work from a home office that enables you to keep an eye on other activities in the house if you need to be involved for a short period. Have established quiet times when your office knows it is okay to contact you at home.
	Keep one or more pictures of friends or family on your desk. Try working from home one day a week and see whether you are still able to be productive. Allow family to call or e-mail you when important. Keep instant messaging on.	If your child is sick or you need to be at home for the repairman on the day of a big meeting at work, rather than taking the whole day off as a personal day, try teleconferencing in for that one occasion and let people know you want to be involved and would rather do this than miss the meeting.
	Bring your kids, spouse, or partners with you on business trips when possible.	If you have a job that will simply pile up while you are away, take one day of vacation to scan e-mail and phone messages, so your first day back at the office is not so overwhelming when you return.
	Take your cell phone into meetings but keep it on vibrate and screen for emergencies.	Keep your cell phone with you when you are at home or running errands, but keep it on vibrate, and if not critical, let callers know you got their calls and will call them back the next day first thing in the morning.
	Take advantage of work events such as families-invited Christmas parties or bring-your-child-to-work day.	Invite coworkers you enjoy to get-togethers at home.
Temporal integration	Vary your work schedule each day in response to family or personal issues. Try to integrate work and family only when it doesn't harm your focus and performance in the other domain.	
	Let family or friends interrupt your work if important.	
	Work at night or on weekends to "catch up" on projects delayed while you were attending to a family or personal issue.	

(continued)

Mental/ emotional integration	Focus on work *and* family or personal life during the day. For example, take a moment to call your kids to make sure they got home from school and are starting homework. Or call your boss if you need to leave early to go to a doctor's appointment to finish up an important work matter so it isn't left undone until the next day.
	Take on more responsibilities around the home for chores and other family needs, if you had been limiting this to focus just on work and had not been carrying your weight at home.
	Discuss your family or personal interests at the office enough to humanize your work interactions but not enough to distract others or hurt your own or their productivity.
	Discuss your work with your family so that they can share in your concerns and accomplishments, but not so much that work-related conversation dominates your home life.
	Give your attention to whatever has the highest priority at the moment.

Exploring Flexstyle Options: Key Tactics for Volleying More Effectively

Those wishing to be more effective in an overall flexstyle comprised of both integration and separation at different times may use the tips related to both of these approaches. You can also use *time triggers*. For most of the Volleyers we interviewed, *time triggers* were used to determine when to separate and when to integrate.

> **TIP #9**
> Establish time triggers to help you transition between segmentation and integration of work and personal or family activities.

Practice letting time dictate when you stop working for the day, if you are separating, and use time and days to set clear rules for when you will integrate. These are called time triggers; you let the clock help you make the transition to move between work and home or vice versa if you have trouble making this move. For example, some people call it a day at 5:00 p.m. If they haven't finished a project or task by then, they come in early the next morning to get it done. If you're a Quality Timer, you may also find these suggestions useful for focusing more sharply on professional or personal responsibilities when you want to. You may decide that Fridays will be your day for integration, working at home, stretching out your workday to accommodate a doctor visit, or other errands.

TIP #10

Redesign workloads at home or work to focus on things you value the most.

If you want to be able to have more quality time at work and home, make sure that the time you spend at work or home is focused on the tasks and activities you value most and are best at. So if you love cooking but hate cleaning the dishes, redesign your home workload so that you get help with the dishes but have more time to cook the gourmet meal. The strategy also can work on the job. If you are great at managing the books, but not so great at the human resource management part of your job, ask your boss if you could redesign your job to increase your workload to focus more on the financial needs of the workgroup. In return you would have someone else do the human resource duties that take you longer but that another person is better at. In this way you are able to get home earlier to have quality time, yet still shine at work by doing what you do best.

Exploring Flexstyle Options—Tactics for Separating More Effectively

In Chapter 2, "Knowing Your Flexstyle," and Chapter 5, "Tradeoffs of Compartmentalizing Work and Personal Life," we described a variety of steps people use to compartmentalize the many dimensions of their lives. Some individuals shape their physical environment—for example, by working only in an office or, if they telecommute, by working only in a space exclusively designated for professional activities. This section offers additional small changes that can help you separate more effectively.

TIP #11

Consciously manage when and with whom you talk about work and personal life.

Limiting discussions about work while you're at home and about family or personal life when you're at work can further help you separate more effectively. Take Anna, a financial consultant at Datatel. Anna works with clients in numerous cities across the United States. This Work Firster has made her career her top priority. She loves her job and rarely discusses family issues with her boss or colleagues during work hours, which allows her to have focused work time and then focused down time when not working.

TIP #12
Know who you are when you are there.

From talking to people like Anna and others, we learned that you can separate more effectively by clarifying which role—professional person, parent, community member, friend, and so forth—you identify with most strongly. Anna has decided to discuss her work-related concerns and accomplishments with her spouse—but not to talk about her personal life at the office—because she strongly identifies herself as a professional person.

Larry provides another example. The leader of a product specialist team and a longtime employee at Infocom, he is divorced, with grown children, and limited family responsibilities. He works from home 99% of the time but is a Work Firster who puts his career first. His ability to separate enables him to be highly productive and to keep his telecommute arrangement. He says:

> *In my situation, I'm not faced with family unless I want to be. I have the luxury of scheduling my day around work or personal.... I have a work ethic that leads me to separate the two. I just never allowed personal life to interfere with my work.*

In deciding how much to separate, you may find it helpful to clarify your core values and priorities. For example, if you're a Work Firster who's having trouble focusing at the office because you're thinking about weekend plans, remind yourself of how important your professional life is to your sense of identity. Or if you're a Family Firster who's feeling guilty that you've left the office to pick up your child from daycare while your colleagues remain in their cubicles, remind yourself of the value you place on being a good parent.

TIP #13
Match your behaviors to your priorities.

Some people separate more effectively by changing their behavior to signal which role—professional or personal—they're focusing on at the moment. British researcher Susanne Tietze described this technique in a study of telecommuters. One participant, Max, worked designated hours from a home office. During his work hours, if he encountered his wife or children, he acted "professionally; that is to say, briefly, but courteously." He reported feeling "uneasy" about using this approach, particularly with his children. Still, he considered it a necessary part of staying focused on work while operating from his home office.[5]

Because more and more people are working from home some of the time, or are more accessible to family and friends when at work due to cell phones, e-mail, and pagers, Table 8.4 summarizes the tactics we've seen people use to separate more effectively when at work or at home. Some of these tips are most applicable for those working from a corporate office; others are most applicable for those working from a remote location or home. Some may prove helpful in either situation.

Table 8.4 *Tactics for Separating More Effectively*

	Separating in a Corporate Office	Separating in a Home Office
Behavioral separation	Adopt a professional demeanor during phone calls or other interactions with friends and family from the office.	Act professionally (briefly, courteously) during work hours when interacting with family or friends.
Physical separation	Work in the office, rather than at home.	Work at home, but with a designated office.
	Avoid taking extra work home.	Have a door to the office.
		Have a separate data and phone line.
		Have separate work and personal e-mail accounts.
Temporal separation	Handle personal matters at the beginning or end of the day so that you stay focused on work for longer stretches of time.	Work set hours each day, as you would in a corporate office.
	Take formal vacation time if needed to deal with unexpected family issues.	Work intensely for eight hours but then stop. Resist the urge to check work-related e-mails after your workday has ended.

	Separating in a Corporate Office	Separating in a Home Office
Mental/ emotional separation	Think about work at the office and personal concerns at home.	Think about work at the office and personal concerns after hours.
	Have a daycare or pet-sitting arrangement you can trust.	Have a daycare or pet-sitting arrangement you can trust.
	Hire someone to do your food shopping, start dinner or laundry, or meet the repairman.	Hire someone to do your food shopping, start dinner or laundry, or meet the repairman.
	Focus on what's critical according to your identity and core values.	Focus on what's critical according to your identity and core values.
	Don't talk about family at work, if work is your priority.	Don't talk about family during work hours or with colleagues, if work is your priority.
	Don't talk about work at home, if home is your priority.	Don't talk about work with family or friends during nonwork hours, if home is your priority.

Conclusion

Changing your flexstyle can involve all three types of specific changes we've described in this chapter—gaining control over the flexibility in your life, working to counter the disadvantages of your current flexstyle, and exploring new options for how to live your flexstyle or a shift to a new one. These specific changes can be implemented with the process of general change introduced in Chapter 7. It doesn't matter whether the changes are small or dramatic—the same principles apply. And just as we argued in Chapter 7, small changes can bring extraordinary results as you begin the journey on the path to change.

Table 8.5 *Summary: Change Strategies Tailored to Specific Flexstyles*

Strategy	Flexstyle	Tip
1. Gaining Control	Reactors	Make others more aware of your life demands. Set access rules. Seek help and resources. Limit multitasking and take mini-breaks.
	Job Warriors	Create substitutes for yourself for tasks you don't value the most. Negotiate to reduce workload or ask for help when overloaded. Create portable virtual integration tactics. Create workable transitions. Consciously choose when you separate and when you integrate.
	Captives	Negotiate to pilot job flexibility. Try out a new flexstyle. Participate in creating organizationwide change toward more flexibility for everyone.
2. Reducing the Disadvantages of Your Current Flexstyle	Family Firster	Contribute unique value at work. Build your reputation.
	Work Firster	Carve out time for family or self. Use time and energy wisely. Keep a time log to spot bad patterns.
	Captive	Find a stress management approach. Don't work on your breaks.
	Quality Timer	Integrate or separate in larger blocks of time to reduce switching costs. Find times to turn off cell phone and instant messaging.
	Job Warrior	Use travel time strategically to ease transitions. Focus on valued activities when at home.
	Fusion Lover	Track hours to identify unhealthy patterns Minimize process losses by reducing constant switching between work and personal life.
		Set dates to revisit your flexstyle and examine stakeholders' satisfaction.

Strategy	Flexstyle	Tip
2. Reducing the Disadvantages of Your Current Flexstyle (continued)	Reactor	Resist the urge to take on more.
		Don't be afraid to say no sometimes.
		Be realistic with yourself and others.
		Reduce the number of daily times you switch back and forth between work and personal life.
3. Exploring New Flexstyles	Tactics for Integrating	Be more available to family, friends and coworkers.
		Focus on the priority of the moment.
		Talk about work and family at home and work.
		Establish new routines and rituals.
	Tactics for Volleying	Establish time triggers to help transitions between segmenting and integrating.
		Redesign workload to focus on what you value.
	Tactics for Separating	Limit cross-domain talk.
		Know who you are when and where you are. Match your behavior to your true priorities.

chapter nine

Negotiating a New Flexstyle and a Life That Works on Your Terms

I work in the main office from 8:00 a.m. until 6:30 p.m. Then I have dinner, watch the news, and then around 9:00 p.m., I head to my home office, where I spend the next two to three hours responding by e-mail to customers' requests for technical support. My company does not pay overtime for professionals even though the work I have to do takes much longer than 40 hours. I don't mind because I have been getting promoted, but I am beginning to wonder whether there is more to life than just work. I am just not sure how to begin to negotiate a different way of living.

Larry, a Work Firster

Negotiation: Finding Your Voice

Larry makes his career his top priority and has a strong work ethic. He focuses entirely on his sales job during the workday and puts in long hours each week by catching up on e-mail at night. With a high desire for privacy, he handles personal obligations after work hours and out of earshot of his colleagues. He is divorced with no children. Fully immersed in his professional responsibilities, Larry hasn't taken time to look into the many formal work-life benefits available at his company—such as personal or sick leave. And those benefits he is aware of haven't appealed much to him. Larry has never thought of himself as someone who needs his employer's help with "balance." Only people with problems or those who lack a strong career orientation have such a need, he believes.

Larry's devotion to his career has paid him big dividends. For example, he has received regular above-average pay increases as well as promotions nearly every two years. Yet recently, he has begun experiencing medical problems, including recurring viral infections that have required frequent visits to his physician. He realized that to take better care of his health, he would need to make some changes in how he allocates his time and energy. But after many years of putting work before his personal life, he wonders whether his employer would be open to change—and whether he himself would be able to "make a change stick."

If Larry hopes to make the adjustments required to maintain both his health and his successful career, he will probably have to exercise what Princeton economist Albert Hirschman and other researchers call his *voice option* and negotiate new arrangements with key individuals.[1] Of course, as some people do, he could simply opt out of corporate life or continue to suffer in silence at his company. But each of these options raises problems. If he left the corporate world, he would have to figure out how to pay for health insurance and other benefits himself, identify other sources of income, and adjust to the many uncertainties associated with self-employment or unemployment. If he stayed with his current employer without broaching the subject of change, he would risk feeling less and less satisfied by and engaged in his work—a painful emotional development that would cost him *and* his company.

For these reasons, negotiation likely constitutes Larry's best option now that he has realized that his flexstyle is no longer serving him well. *Negotiation* is a process by which two people work through differences in their needs or interests and arrive at an agreement that satisfies both of them. Through negotiation, the participants present offers and counteroffers, and make concessions and compromises to resolve their differences.[2]

Yet many people hesitate to use negotiation. Some fear that if they ask for a different deal, their boss will overlook them when future opportunities—for example, a high-profile overseas assignment or a chance to lead an exciting new project—come along. Others have an intense need to please their boss and thereby win her approval. Rocking the work-life boat, they assume, will only annoy their supervisor. Still others simply cannot envision any other way of working and living than the one they see their colleagues using. Immersed in their organization's culture, they've absorbed its values and norms, and they assume that "this is the way we do things here."

In this chapter, we offer ideas for overcoming such mental obstacles to productive negotiation, illustrated with real examples from individuals who have successfully bargained for flexstyle changes. We focus on two simple but critical ideas that could help you to negotiate changes to your own flexstyle—*preparation* and *collaboration*. Seasoned negotiators know that the time you devote to preparing for negotiation not only can help you overcome any hesitancy or anxiety you might feel about bargaining but also can mean the difference between success and failure. After you are prepared to negotiate, you'll need to engage in the process, and we cover the choices you have about how to bargain. A collaborative approach, where you not only consider your own needs but also try to craft a deal that benefits others is most often going to work best when you try to change your flexstyle.

Because negotiation can be useful in helping you to mitigate or reduce constraints on how you manage your priorities, this chapter will prove particularly helpful if you currently see yourself as someone who is generally unhappy with how you are managing relationships between work and personal life: Reactor, Job Warrior, or Captive trapped in an inflexible job. As you've seen, these flexstyles are characterized by a sense of limited control and feelings of regret, frustration, and stress. But even if you are largely happy with your style—a Fusion Lover, Quality Timer, or Firster—you can also benefit from the negotiation techniques offered in this chapter.

Larry's story is a case in point: Though he's generally happy with being a Work Firster, his medical problems have forced him to make some changes. And because he had some concerns about how his employer would respond to his request for new working arrangements, negotiation offers the most promising route to crafting a life that works more on his terms. Let's take a closer look at his story to distill lessons for how you, too, might negotiate positive change.

The New Deal Larry Wants

Working long hours from the corporate office didn't enable Larry to compartmentalize his professional and personal life as much as he wanted—especially after he began experiencing health problems that required frequent visits to his physician. He particularly didn't want his coworkers and bosses to know about his medical concerns, because he worried that they would view him as less effective on the job. If his boss had questions about his effectiveness, he thought, she might withhold the salary increases and promotions that had meant so much to him over the years.

But it was hard to keep his medical situation private. Larry realized that colleagues could sometimes overhear him as he made appointments to see his physician. And naturally, they asked where he had been when they saw him returning to the office after a doctor's visit. To keep these incidents to a minimum, he began postponing making medical appointments until days he could afford to take a half day off. That meant he wasn't always taking care of himself the way that his doctor wanted. Combined with the limited exercise he was allowing himself, these sporadic appointments seriously undermined his long-term health. Larry had long enjoyed being a Work Firster who kept professional and personal commitments strictly separate, yet he decided that adopting a flexstyle more like that of a Quality Timer would help him take better care of his health—and, therefore, his on-the-job performance. The flexibility of volleying—shifting as needed between integrating and separating work and nonwork priorities—strongly appealed to him.

One major way Larry could put a Quality Timer strategy into action was to integrate his doctors' appointments more flexibly into his regular workday. Sure, he always had this as an option, but he had established the expectation—in himself, his boss, and his colleagues—that he would be in the office five days a week from 8:00 a.m. to 6:30 p.m—no matter what. The time had come to rethink this expectation. Though he had effected some changes himself—for example, scheduling medical appointments during vacation half-days—these tactics had yielded less-than-optimal results. Not only was he scheduling less frequent appointments than he needed, but he had also begun to resent sacrificing his vacation time for medical matters. This resentment sometimes led him to cancel or reschedule appointments—which only put his health at further risk.

Larry decided that working one day a week from home would help him resolve his dilemma. With this arrangement, he could continue focusing just as much on work as he always had, while also maintaining privacy regarding his health. He could schedule his medical visits on work-from-home days largely over his lunch hour, which he rarely took anyway, or late in the afternoon, when he would normally be commuting. This plan would also enable him to stop using vacation or personal days for medical appointments. Excited as he was by the thought of making a positive change, Larry still felt unsure about how it would go when he presented his case to his employer.

During the rest of this chapter, we share tips and tools that you and other people like Larry can use to negotiate creating a better working life. You can use these tactics with key players from either your work or private life from whom you need support to initiate your new flexstyle.

Preparation Negotiation Tactics

TIP #1
Know thyself.

"Know thyself" is good advice for negotiators. Indeed, the importance of understanding your own goals and priorities constitutes a central theme in this book. Before you can broach the subject of change with your boss, colleague, or family member, you must first clarify what you want. Ask yourself questions like: In my view, what's the ideal way to manage my work and nonwork priorities? What changes must I make to achieve that ideal? What's the least amount of change I could live with? What are my best options if the other person doesn't agree to my proposed plan for change?

For example, suppose that for the past few years you've had primary responsibility for managing your household. While your spouse has focused on his career, you've had a respectable but low-pressure job that enabled you to take charge of everything related to the house. You've made appointments with and overseen the work of service professionals such as landscapers, plumbers, and painters. You've paid the bills, called the phone company to straighten out overdue notices, and done all the grocery shopping, cooking, and cleaning. Now you have an opportunity to take a big step up at your company—in the form of a promotion that will demand a lot more concentration from you on the job. You want to put work first so that you can take advantage of this new opportunity. But you know this won't go over too well with your spouse, who won't be interested in or able to take on more household management responsibilities. Here's how you might answer the previous questions:

- **In my view, what's the ideal way to manage my work and nonwork priorities?** Right now, I want to focus enough on my career to take advantage of the advancement opportunity my employer is offering me.

- **What changes must I make to achieve that ideal?** I need to work late most nights for the next six months, so I can get up to speed on my new responsibilities.

- **What's the least amount of change I could live with?** At the very least, I need two nights a week that I can work late if necessary to get control of new projects.

- **What are my best options if the other person doesn't agree to my proposed plan for change?** Perhaps I could use the salary increase that will come with my promotion to hire someone to help with shopping, cleaning, and other household responsibilities. Or we could get takeout on some nights to reduce the amount of shopping, cooking, and cleaning that needs to be done.

These questions can be adapted to other flexstyles. For example, suppose you're a Job Warrior who wants more quality time at work and home during certain parts of the year. If your job requires you to travel during most of the year, perhaps you can make arrangements with your boss or clients not to travel at all during the last half of August, when your entire family gets together every year for a reunion. However, to reassure your boss of your reliability, you agree to be available by phone to clients during business hours if needed during those two weeks. By negotiating this relatively small change, you not only get what you want, but you also reaffirm for your boss that you're still the "go to" person he can rely on 100% of the year.

Sometimes "knowing thyself" means re-examining long-held assumptions about the roles you play in your personal or professional life. For example, let's say you're the one daughter in a family with three sons, and you've taken the lead in caring for your aging mother, despite a demanding career. This care includes visiting your mother at least once a day in her home across town, bringing her groceries, and helping her with her finances. You want to devote more time and energy to your career, but you don't see a way to do this without cutting back on the amount of time you spend helping your mother. As long as you believe that it's the responsibility of a daughter to care for an aging parent and that only you can provide the best possible care, you'll find it difficult to negotiate shared responsibility with your brothers or explore other solutions, such as hiring caregivers. Before you can bargain for a new arrangement, you need to challenge your assumptions about who's "supposed to take care of Mom," what it means to be a "good daughter," and whether your brothers or someone else could possibly provide assistance and attention that are just as good as what you provide.

We can fall into similar traps in work-related roles. For instance, let's say you believe you're the only person in your department who can do a particular task well—such as making sales pitches to potential new customers or fixing computer problems. In this case, you won't likely negotiate a change that enables you to free up more time for long-neglected personal obligations—even if handling that particular on-the-job task is putting you at risk for burnout.

The lesson? Before negotiating new work-life arrangements, you may sometimes need to challenge—and let go of—the assumptions behind your current strategy. Let's return to Larry's case. To get his new deal, he needed to challenge two assumptions. He had to let go of his own view that he always had to do his medical appointments on his personal time. Second, he had to let go of his view that his company would let no one—not even top performers—telecommute one day a week. This brings us to our next tip—don't be afraid to ask for what you need and assume things will get nasty if you do.

TIP #2
Don't be afraid to ask or assume things will get nasty if you do.

One common misconception about negotiation is that it is necessarily a tough, confrontational, and unpleasant process. For example, perhaps you associate negotiation with those uncomfortable times you've haggled over the purchase price of a new car or house, when you felt certain that the salesperson wasn't telling you the whole truth or was trying to manipulate you. In these types of negotiations, it's natural to conclude that you have to be tough as nails to prevent "the other guy" from taking advantage of you. And you probably assume that after the dust settles, there's going to be a winner and a loser. For many people, this unsavory picture of negotiation is enough to prevent them from even considering bargaining with their boss to better mesh their work and personal lives.

There are different ways to negotiate—many of them principled and civil. Any incipient nastiness tends to evaporate as soon as both parties take the attitude that they will be crafting an agreement that satisfies both of them—and that they will each come out a winner. Larry did this by developing a proposal that highlighted how his proposed work-from-home arrangement would benefit his company in terms of measurable increases in his productivity.

Moreover, negotiations don't have to be complex and harrowing odysseys. Sometimes a quick bit of deal-making is all that's needed to get the results you want—whether it's suggesting to your boss that you participate in an important upcoming meeting by conference phone to save time, or telling your spouse that you'll take out the garbage for the next three weeks if she deals with the plumber today so that you can attend a corporate function. In Larry's case, his negotiation was no big deal to his boss, and even though Larry fixated for weeks on how to ask, his boss was more than willing to experiment with a good performer.

TIP #3
Don't assume your employer will take the initiative.

Today, many people work in organizations that put them under constant pressure to deliver top performance. This pressure makes it easy for people—especially

Work Firsters—to place work priorities so far ahead of personal needs that eventually burnout ensues. Under these conditions, the do-it-yourself change tactics discussed in earlier chapters may not be enough to achieve a flexstyle that works in a positive way for you. Instead, some changes in job structure or organizational policies may be in order. And those require negotiation.

Don't assume that your employer will take the initiative in crafting positive solutions to your work-life dilemmas. Many organizations believe that it's up to individual employees to resolve such dilemmas themselves. Already-busy managers aren't likely to think proactively about what changes might help their direct reports or colleagues better manage the many commitments in their lives.

For these reasons, like Larry, you will probably need to initiate negotiations for change—even though in the short run it would be much easier to let things drift along without rocking the boat. Though doing so may seem daunting, keep in mind that you'll be far more likely to get the changes you want by broaching the subject yourself than you will by waiting for your supervisor to recognize that a problem exists and to offer solutions.

TIP #4
Do your homework.

Research on negotiation shows that preparations made before the bargaining even begins can influence the outcome just as strongly as the negotiation tactics used at the table.[3] The more you prepare yourself, the more confident you will feel and the more successful you are likely to be in any negotiation.

Accordingly, before broaching the subject of working from home to his boss, Larry did his homework. He listed all the reasons that his plan would benefit the company by further enhancing his already impressive productivity. For example, he would save on commuting time on the days he worked from home. Therefore, he could start handling work-related tasks earlier in the morning and continue working later into the afternoon and evening if needed. He was currently commuting nearly an hour each way to and from the office—time that he was not spending on work. The beginning of the week was typically the busiest in the sales department, so Larry also developed an argument showing how working from home on Fridays would fit comfortably with the department's typical rhythm. In addition, he prepared reports showing how his performance track record compared to that of peers and offered ideas for how colleagues and customers could easily reach him on work-from-home days.

Larry's diligence paid off. He presented his proposed plan to his supervisor, who allowed him to pilot the plan for several months. At the end of the pilot, his supervisor was convinced that the arrangement was not only helping Larry but also enabling him to spend more time than ever satisfying clients' needs—while being just as reachable and responsive as always. The supervisor approved the new arrangement for the long term. Larry, his coworkers, and the company's clients all saw that Larry could be counted on to deliver—even from a home office. The notion of working from home one day a week, utterly novel at Larry's company, turned out to be no big deal.

With his new arrangement, Larry became a Quality Timer who separates during the days he's at the corporate office and integrates during the days he works from home. Larry is pleased with his new flexstyle. He not only maintains his privacy, but he's also taking better care of his health while delivering higher-than-ever performance on the job. "[I've] just never allowed personal life to interfere with my work," he notes. "[But] when I need to use time to go to the doctor, I feel more comfortable doing that from home than explaining to people around the office."

TIP #5
Be ready to listen for your wake-up call.

Critical life events can serve as a wake-up call—putting us on notice that it's time to negotiate a change and helping us overcome any reluctance toward negotiation. Such an event may take the form of a medical crisis, the death of a parent, or some other loss that reminds you how short life really is. Children's departure for college, a major milestone birthday, or the simple realization that you're deeply unhappy with your career or personal life (or both) can also catalyze a willingness to change.

Sally is a highly regarded professor at a prestigious Ivy League university. She consults frequently to U.S. and foreign governments and prestigious research think tanks. As she built her career, her husband ran his own successful business, and they hired a nanny to help them raise their two children. For years, Sally put in brutally long hours, even handling work projects while attending her children's swim meets and while on vacations. She was a Reactor—allowing work to bleed into her family and personal life because she felt she had no choice if she hoped to construct and maintain a successful career.

Last year, a number of events prompted Sally to reconsider her flexstyle. For one thing, she turned 40—a milestone birthday that prompted her to take stock of her life and to notice, for the first time, how stressful things had become. In addition, her mother died. Sally had been close to her mother, who passed away a week before the entire family was scheduled to go on a much-anticipated vacation. Around this difficult time, Sally also developed some minor health problems, including leg cramps while sitting at the computer. Simultaneously, she became more sharply aware of the fact that her high-school-aged children would soon be leaving for college. She realized that there was little time remaining when she would have ready access to them. Equally unsettling, she admitted to herself that she wasn't satisfied with her life overall, despite her success "on paper."

Meanwhile, Sally's husband and children began complaining about the amount of time she devoted to her work. She was often late picking up the kids from school. Her son had taken to telling her to turn off the computer 15 minutes before they had to go somewhere, to help her overcome her addiction to e-mail and boost the chances that the family would arrive at their destinations on time. One evening, her husband asked her to go with him to a Tuesday-night concert. When Sally declined, citing the need to catch up on work, the two had an intense argument.

Spurred by painful losses, unsettling realizations, and escalating family tensions, Sally decided to change to a Quality Timer flexstyle. This new flexstyle, she reasoned, would let her switch between integrating and separating as needed to tend to her professional and family commitments in more equal measure. She negotiated with her family to seek a job at another university where the work would present far less pressure. Even though they regretted losing the higher salary and prestige that had come with her being at an Ivy League university, she persuaded them to agree to the job change by pointing out that it would vastly improve the quality of their family life.

She also bargained for her family's assistance in carving out more time for herself. She made it clear that just because she was moving to a less-demanding job, it didn't mean that she would now devote 100% of her free time to catering to her husband and children—providing gourmet meals every night, doing all the housework, and so forth. She needed time for her own interests as well, she explained. To that end, she joined a book club and a tennis group, two activities that she loved but had given up for many years. In addition, every Friday she stopped work at 4:00 p.m., so she could spend time on both family and personal commitments. For instance, she used her newly liberated time to organize her family's digital photos. She also went for a walk every day at noon with a colleague instead of working through lunch. She found herself enjoying the companionship and noticed that her leg cramps disappeared.

Despite her more relaxed pace on the job, Sally maintained her professional stature; however, she eliminated the negative consequences of her previous flexstyle—including switching costs, letting her job creep into her personal and family life, and risking burnout. Thanks to the new arrangements she negotiated with her family, she was taking better care of herself and her loved ones while also sustaining her professional success.

TIP #6
Know the other guy's interests.

Just as you must identify your own goals, interests, and damaging assumptions before entering into a negotiation, you need to do your homework to discern the other party's priorities. Ask yourself: How will they likely respond to my proposed plan for change? How will the change affect them—both positively and negatively? What worries will they likely have? Are there any interests that we both share and that we could, therefore, serve by crafting a mutually satisfying solution?

Consider Jeff, an IT support staffer who services a large university department. He had arranged his work life so that people in the department had his cell phone number and could call him on weekends and throughout the night if they needed him to fix a computer problem. As a result, he had no life outside work. Realizing that he couldn't go on this way indefinitely, Jeff decided to make some changes. In particular, he wanted to designate some work-free times during the weekends so that he could spend time getting together with friends and pursuing other long-neglected interests.

Before initiating discussions about his desire for change, he identified potential concerns of his in-house "clients" and brainstormed ideas for addressing those concerns. For example, he guessed that the department staffers would be highly uncomfortable if they thought they couldn't contact him at all over the weekend. They were too used to his being available at any time. To address this concern, he let his colleagues know that if an IT problem cropped up over the weekend, they could reach him at his office between 5:00 p.m. and 7:00 p.m. on Sunday. With his clients, he also worked out a crystal-clear definition of what constituted an emergency—an IT problem that required his attention. And he established an online "redbook," in which clients logged computer problems on a special Web site and prioritized them as "urgent" (they could not continue their work until the problem was fixed) or as "low priority" (they could continue their work, but the problem would still need to be fixed by a certain date).

Jeff's careful analysis of his clients' concerns paid off: He was able to negotiate a solution that works for both him and his clients. He is still available to them for emergencies, and clients know they can still reach him if needed over the weekend. But now he has more control over when he responds to a client. He can review the online redbook and e-mail clients to buy himself time and provide an estimate of when he'll fix the problem. And by answering e-mail and checking the redbook when he chooses to (rather than responding in a knee-jerk manner every time a client pages him), he has more time for nonwork interests.

Discerning the other party's interests like Jeff and Larry did can help you overcome any reluctance to negotiating that you may feel. For instance, if you're a Job Warrior, you may find it easier to get on a plane and fly across the country to attend a two-hour client meeting than to ask your boss whether you can teleconference in once in a while. Perhaps you assume that your boss will view your request as a sign of diminishing commitment to the job. To challenge this assumption, articulate in your own mind the value that you bring to the table—and that your boss cares most about. In this example, that value is your ability to cultivate positive relationships with customers. Sure, relationship-building requires some degree of face-to-face contact—particularly in the early stages of a relationship and when dealing with certain problems that must be handled onsite. When you've established a solid relationship, an occasional teleconference won't hurt the bonds you've built with important customers. The key is to determine when a teleconference is acceptable and to communicate your reasoning.

Collaboration Tactics

TIP #7
Craft "integrative" (win-win) bargains.

After you reflect on what you are looking for, how your proposed plan might affect those around you, and what you think they are looking for, you are ready to initiate a conversation about the changes you want to make. In the world of negotiations, bargainers use two main approaches. *Distributive bargaining* is the classic adversarial process where is it assumed that one party wins and one party loses.[4] During distributive bargaining, participants disguise their interests and priorities, look out only for their own welfare, and try to grab the most value from the deal at the expense of their "opponent." The other approach, popularized in books such as Fisher and Ury's *Getting to Yes!*, is often termed *integrative bargaining*, which is commonly known as a win-win type of bargaining.[5] So instead of viewing the negotiation as a process where one party generally wins and the other loses, during integrative bargaining, you work with other parties, such as your boss or coworkers, to problem solve and identify outcomes from supporting change to a new flexstyle that would make both you and them better off.

For example, say you want to not work weekends or evenings during the summer months so that you can participate in training for a marathon even though most employees do some after-hours work in the summer. If you bargain for this without identifying the interests of others you work with, they might view this negotiation as win-lose. But if you offer to provide after-hours coverage during some workdays adjacent to holidays such as Thanksgiving or Easter in return for time off in the summer, it is likely that you have come up with a win-win solution for yourself and the company.

So integrative or win-win bargaining is the way to go when you want to negotiate with others to let you adjust your flexstyle. It does require you to win the other person's trust and to come up with creative ideas for solving your conflicts.

How do you get to win-win solutions? The first thing you must do is think of the other parties' interests. We always go into negotiations thinking of what we want. Instead we need to focus on what *the others want* in the framing of how we ask what *we* want.

TIP #8
Avoid creating more work for your boss and address the bosses greatest fears.

Our research on managers' reactions to flexible work arrangements offers many lessons—particularly for Captives who want to craft less-rigid work arrangements that afford them a more workable life. In particular, many managers have mixed feelings about flexible work arrangements. They may believe that such arrangements will burden them with even more work than they're already shouldering.

For example, scheduling meetings for direct reports who all work different hours may strike them as a nightmare.

Yet you can overcome your manager's resistance to new work deals. For example, help your manager and coworkers agree on core hours during which all team members will be available for meetings. Decide together when it's okay for particular team members to participate in such meetings by phone. And define what constitutes an emergency and when it's acceptable to call employees at home. By articulating these details, you reassure your manager that new work arrangements won't add inordinately to his responsibilities.

Some managers feel particularly uncomfortable with work arrangements that prevent them from directly overseeing their employees. Indeed, many managers view their primary responsibility as closely monitoring and controlling employees' work. For these supervisors, work-from-home arrangements give them the sense of losing control over this central responsibility. To regain that control, such managers believe they will have to take on extra work—including phoning or e-mailing direct reports more frequently to check up on them. In such cases, you can reduce your boss's concerns about loss of control and extra work by agreeing to check in with her regularly to report on your work progress. (Broader cultural change in the organization may also be required to address this concern—something we explore in Chapter 10, "Not Going It Alone: Making Sustainable Change at Your Workplace.")

Consider Sheila, a Quality Timer, who won her boss's approval to work at home during part of the week by mitigating his worries about how he would assess her productivity. "In this department, if you need to work at home, you can. It's left up to you, as long as you don't abuse it," Sheila explains. The rules of their arrangement include "The boss must have a way to reach you," and "You'll be judged by the outcomes of your work, not the number of hours you're at your desk." At Sheila's company, permission to work from home "depends on your manager and your department." Thus the company is "kind of schizophrenic on the whole idea." In such organizations, work-from-home arrangements may remain tenuous unless the number of such arrangements reaches such a critical mass that it begins reshaping the company's overall culture.

TIP #9
Find allies.

Published studies have shown that managers can use several tactics to "sell" their superiors on their ideas for enacting change in their workplaces.[6] These tactics include making the business case for your desired change, complete with supporting facts and evidence. Finding allies can also be useful. Presenting a well-thought-out proposal from a coalition of individuals—showing how everyone in the work group or department would similarly benefit from flexible hours and providing a clear plan for coordinating work—can be more persuasive than presenting a plan for just one person. To mitigate any chance that your boss might feel you're "ganging up on" him, always frame your proposal in terms of how the company will benefit—in enhanced productivity, higher profits, or some other measurable outcome.

TIP #10
Negotiate new deals with family.

Negotiating new arrangements in the workplace may also require effecting changes at home. For example, if you've won approval to work from home several days a week, you may have to craft agreements with family members to ensure that they know when it's okay to interrupt you during telecommuting days. Yet many people have difficulty associating family with negotiation. We care so much about our family members and loved ones and need them so much that it might seem odd or uncomfortable for you to think about trying to "bargain" with them. Instead, we often think of ourselves as "asking family members for help" in handling our many responsibilities. Nonetheless, whether you view work-life discussions with family as negotiating or asking for help, you still need to apply certain principles of effective bargaining to design mutually beneficial arrangements.

By studying workers in their homes, British researcher Suzanne Tietze gained a unique perspective on the kinds of work-from-home deals people strike with family members and how they negotiate those arrangements.[7] Max, a 40-year-old project manager who works from home two days a week, provides one example. Max is married to Emily, and they have two children: four-year-old John and seven-year-old Christina. To devise a successful work-from-home arrangement, Max has made it clear that he does not appreciate interruptions from family or friends while he's on the job. Emily's role is to ensure that the children respect his preference. As a family, they have developed systems to maintain a clear separation between work and home. For instance, a red flag on Max's office door signals that he cannot be disturbed, while a white flag indicates that he is taking a break and will allow interruptions. Max also uses the phrase "Pretend I'm not here" to convey his wish to be left out of some domestic activities.[8]

Max is clearly a Work Firster. With his family, he has negotiated crystal-clear boundaries (physical, behavioral, temporal, and cognitive) so that everyone understands the rules governing how and when he works and the conditions under which he's available to his family. He has had to win Emily's cooperation, in particular, to make this arrangement work. One reason he has succeeded here is that he relies on Emily to be a "gatekeeper," where she is the individual who manages the family so that no one disturbs Max while he is working, a role that fits her interests as well as Max's. Emily doesn't mind her part of the bargain. In fact, she sees her ability to manage the children and to help Max stay focused on work as an important contribution to her family.

Separators often find that after they've established the "ground rules," family members have little difficulty following them. Negotiating rules for integrating can present more of a challenge. Consider Tom, another participant in Tietze's study. Tom is 39 years old and lives with his wife, Sarah, and their three-year-old son, Peter. An international project manager, Tom works from home two to three days per week. Through discussions with his family, he has created an office space, equipped with computer, faxes, and shelves, at one end of the living room area. The office is cluttered with Peter's toys and family CDs. Moreover, Sarah has stored her housekeeping files on the computer and uses it for both domestic management and leisure activities. Tom and his family discussed and agreed together that he would work in this manner so that he could blend work and family activities and feel more a part of household activities. Sometimes Sarah sits down at the computer when Tom takes a coffee break in the kitchen. In such instances, priority is given to the more urgent task, whether domestic or work-related. While at work in his home office, Tom is frequently interrupted, particularly during days when Peter is not at nursery school. At such times, he must frequently renegotiate rules about play times with his son.[9]

Tom's situation illustrates the fact that Integrators—whether Fusion Lovers or Reactors—may find it especially difficult to establish *and* maintain clear ground rules with family. That's because Integrators can't rely on simple rules like "Don't interrupt between 9:00 a.m. and 5:00 p.m.," or "Don't knock whenever there's a red tie on the door." Instead there is much more variability in their work and home lives. Integrators and their families must constantly assess what constitutes the highest priority at any one moment and decide whether being interrupted at work is acceptable. The continual decision making can be difficult for a child to understand. If you're a Fusion Lover, be prepared to frequently renegotiate ground rules you've established. If you neglect to do so, you risk losing control over your flexstyle—and becoming a frustrated Reactor.

There is some good news related to bargaining with your family members. It's more likely that because you care about each other, you'll be able to negotiate in a collaborative fashion.[10] However, remember that it can also be tempting to put your spouse's or partner's interests ahead of your own, out of fear that conflict will damage the relationship. Sacrificing your interests leads only to outcomes that are not mutually beneficial—and therefore not likely sustainable. So do look out for your partner and family's interests, but don't forget to also safeguard your own.

Final Thoughts

Now that you've learned how to negotiate a new flexstyle deal for yourself, don't forget to make it stick. Don't fall into the trap of going back to old, familiar routines and habits. For example, suppose you've struck a deal in which your colleagues have agreed to stop contacting you during off-hours to discuss projects. You can't stop them from sending you e-mails over the weekend, but you've made it clear that you won't respond to the messages until the workweek resumes. Yet, here you are, on a rainy Sunday morning, sitting at your computer. It's too wet outside to do the yard projects you had lined up for the weekend, so you dash off a quick response to a teammate who had sent you an urgent e-mail on Saturday night. You tell yourself, "I'm not going to get anything else done today, so I might as well make myself useful and take care of this project question now."

Falling back into old habits is understandable—but risky. If you do it enough, you'll ultimately experience the same frustration and resentment you felt before you negotiated the new arrangement. You'll also send mixed messages to the people with whom you've negotiated your new deal. In effect, you're telling them you're not that serious about making a change after all. And the next time you propose a new plan to them, they may take your cue and not give your proposal serious consideration.

To make new deals stick, it's vital to reinforce them through your own new behaviors. Consider Larry, who now works from home every Friday to manage his health appointments. To make sure that his new flexstyle delivers its promised benefits, he takes a 10-minute break every two hours, during which he throws in a load of laundry, takes out the garbage, checks out headlines on CNN, or takes a chicken breast out of the freezer to defrost for dinner. He used to do such tasks on the weekends and in the evenings, leaving himself little time for more interesting pursuits. Now evenings and weekends are much less stressful than before. And because Larry has freed up time during the evenings, he's also cooking at home more—a much healthier alternative to his earlier practice of getting takeout dinners almost every night. On work-from-home days when he doesn't have a lunch-time medical appointment, Larry walks his dog around the neighborhood block during the middle of the day. These brisk walks revitalize him and enable him to spend time with his beloved pet. They've also helped him take off a bit of the weight he had gained. Equally important, Larry's new flexstyle has enabled him to work more efficiently. With fewer interruptions and less time spent commuting, he gets more done in less time and has even cut several hours from his workweek.

We have explored changes you can make on your own and negotiation tactics you can use with bosses and family members to change your flexstyle and have a better quality of life. Table 9.1 summarizes the top 10 negotiation tips. In Chapter 10, we shift focus to ways in which you can help your employees, coworkers, and even your family members enact flexstyles that help them feel good about their work and personal life relationships. We also provide suggestions for crafting an organizational culture that embraces workable living. These suggestions range from managing your team or department in new ways to persuading top management to adopt companywide policies that support a diversity of flexstyles. By tackling change on an individual, departmental, and organizational level, you play a vital role in enabling people to achieve fulfilling lives on all fronts—and in helping your organization reap the resulting benefits.

Table 9.1   *Top 10 Tips for Negotiating a New Flexstyle*

Prepare! Prepare! Prepare!	1. Know thyself.
	2. Don't be afraid to ask or don't assume that things will get nasty if you do.
	3. Don't assume your employer will take the initiative.
	4. Do your homework.
	5. Be ready to listen for your wake-up call.
	6. Know "the other guy's interests."
Collaborate!	7. Craft "integrative" (win-win) bargains.
	8. Avoid creating more work for your boss and address the bosses greatest fears.
	9. Find allies.
	10. Negotiate new deals with family.

chapter ten

Not Going It Alone: Making Sustainable Change at Your Workplace

---

The flexibility policies in my organization "[are] anarchistic. There are no rules at all. It's an as needed basis. It should be formalized, so it is not seen as a favor to do so." If you are disciplined, you should be able to work from home. I'd rather construct a policy that works for the majority and deal with the minority separately and try to let my own people telecommute part time whenever they need it. Yet I feel sometimes frustrated in my own job since I don't have permission to work at home, even though I allow my staff to telecommute. It is wishful thinking that if I do this for my staff, maybe someone will do it for me. My boss accepts it grudgingly. I could work from home half of my time.

Dave, Enlightened Infocom Department Manager

Taking the Risk to Establish New Norms at Your Workplace

One of the problems many of the people we spoke with had in forming a new flexstyle was that there were ambiguous rules at their workplace regarding how people were expected to manage work and home. Even when managers like Dave try to be open to letting people control their flexibility, he himself is captive and faces barriers to accessing flexibility in his own job. Take the familiar scenario.

You are a manager of a small group of professionals and work long hours as a Job Warrior. You were planning to work from home on Friday afternoon, so you wouldn't have to fight the weekend traffic and would be able to go to out to dinner early to celebrate your partner's birthday at a local restaurant. You want to try to make up for the many dinners you have missed the last few months. On Wednesday, a colleague with whom you are working closely on a project lets you know that he thinks it is important to schedule a key meeting at 3:00 p.m. Friday. You know one reason he is requesting the meeting is so that he can leave for a long-planned vacation and not have to take work with him. He is a Captive and has worked long hours for you, and once he leaves the office for vacation, he really needs a break to be out of touch for the next week. What do you do?

Like most of us, you probably have faced a situation where your flexstyle doesn't easily mesh with others at work. These dilemmas occur when our work-life needs conflict with those of our customers, boss, or coworkers. When faced with this problem, most of us try to go it alone, negotiating and navigating one-on-one deals incrementally each time a conflict occurs. What makes it worse is that many of us work for companies that have been vague about when workers should and shouldn't be "on duty" and about norms regarding managing work and life relationships. And typically, most companies do prefer to stay out of the work-life norm debate for professionals, unless there is a major deadline or a serious performance problem involving abuse of flexibility. It benefits productivity to keep things vague so that conscientious people will work as long as it takes to get their ever-rising daily workloads done.

If so, the self-management and negotiation strategies discussed in Chapter 7, "Changes Everyone Can Make to Improve Quality of Life," Chapter 8, "Tailoring Change to Your Particular Flexstyle," and Chapter 9, "Negotiating a New Flexstyle and a Life That Works on Your Terms," foster only so much change over the long run. That's because workplace cultures and systems are more powerful than individuals or one-time work arrangements negotiated between an employee and her boss or colleagues. So over the long term, most of us won't find it easy to sustain personal change in how we want to manage relationships between work and family if we try to do it on our own. To make change stick, you must view your flexstyle in the context of the people you work with and your organizational culture and then act. You need to be part of the solution not only for yourself but also for others. You *can* make the workplace better for others at the same time as you help yourself. In fact, it will help you in the long run to be able to sustain your own preferred flexstyle if others feel they can follow their preferred flexstyle. If having a healthy flexstyle comes at the expense of others, or if we have a healthy flexstyle but many others don't, then we will work in unhealthy systems or in systems of backlash and resentment. So don't stop with trying to negotiate change only for yourself. *Remember you are the CEO of your life. You have the power to begin to make changes—even small ones to bring out extraordinary gains—not only for yourself but also for those you work with!*

But how you ask. The solutions offered in this chapter are organized into four themes:

- Clean up your own backyard and neighborhood.
- Understand the challenges of those in most need.
- Engage in dialogue to change attitudes and culture.
- Improve work processes.

Clean Up Your Own Backyard and Neighborhood

We envision change leadership through two metaphors: cleaning up your own backyard (effecting change in how you interact with your peers at work) and cleaning up your neighborhood (lobbying upper management for new organizationwide policies and overall culture change that respects employees' personal needs). In the following sections, we examine each of these more closely.

Cleaning Up Your Backyard

To "clean up your backyard," you change the way people in your own department work—enabling them to use the flexstyles that best suit their needs while also delivering value to the organization. Through these means, you create a *microculture*—the culture of your work unit or department—that supports a diversity of flexstyles. You can also catalyze positive change by understanding how your own flexstyle affects those you work with and then making needed adjustments. By creating a microculture that supports other flexstyles, you may even plant seeds for broader change in your organization. Other groups with whom your team interacts may begin making similar changes after they see the benefits of enabling a diversity of flexstyles.

If you work in an organization where individual managers have little chance of successfully lobbying the executive team for new policies, or if the overall organizational culture does not respect employees' needs for schedule control and social support for personal needs, cleaning up your own backyard becomes even more important.

So let's return to the opening vignette of this chapter. What do you do when your flexstyle preferences conflict with others? Drawing on the negotiation principles we discussed, you need to build trust so that the individual will engage in problem solving to support your and his interests. Because both of you have worked long hours and both have legitimate needs, you can agree with your colleague that the meeting can be held and the work done so that he can go on vacation as planned, but you either request it be held earlier in the day so that you can still take the train home or see whether you can have a virtual meeting and call in. Both of these solutions get the work done but respect each other's needs for schedule control. And in this process of listening to and respecting personal needs, you create allies and begin the change process of respect for diversity of flexstyles.

Cleaning Up Your Neighborhood

In addition to altering the culture of your own group, you can foster broader cultural change—"cleaning up your neighborhood"—by educating top executives on the importance of supporting preferred flexstyles and persuading them to enact new companywide policies that support a diversity of flexstyles. You're especially well positioned to engineer change on this front if you have extensive credibility, positive working relationships with upper management and your peers, and compelling data at hand. For this reason, you may need to make a calculated assessment of which cultural-change approach—backyard, neighborhood, or both—you're ideally suited to lead. Our research has revealed that change can come from the top down, from the grassroots up, or from both directions. Change may prove most enduring if it comes from both top and bottom. Why? A new enterprisewide policy designed to support greater flexibility (think flextime, job sharing, or reduced workload) is useless unless people take advantage of it. And often, employees won't use such a policy if their team's or department's microculture says "You won't get anywhere in this company unless you sacrifice everything for the job."

Before we introduce specific change tactics for cleaning up your backyard and neighborhood, let's take a closer look at the types of problematic management cultures that can prevent you, your colleagues, or your employees from building workable lives. These cultures can infuse an entire organization (*macrocultures*) as well as individual departments and teams (*microcultures*). By understanding these problem cultures, you can more easily decide how best to lead the way toward healthy flexstyles in your own organization.

Understand the Challenges of Those in Most Need

Our research suggests that a *management culture*—the assumptions and values that guide day-to-day rituals, workplace norms, and general conditions in a work unit or organization—can erect barriers to a workable life. If you are a Reactor, Captive, or Job Warrior, chances are you already have an understanding of the problems management culture can create because you're one of the people struggling with a culture that just doesn't support the kind of flexstyle you want. Reactors struggle with having control over the volume and timing of demands, often from both work and home. At work, this is typically driven by working in an organization where there is too much integration and where an expectation has developed that workers will be always available. Job Warriors labor in firms where they are swamped with overwork and expected to put their work ahead of their personal needs, at least during periods of travel or peak work. And Captives face cultures that enforce separation between work and home. These three problem cultures—too much integration, being forced to choose between work and personal life, and enforced separation—can prevent you from moving toward the flexstyle you desire and can complicate your efforts to make broader changes in your firm. But armed with insight into how these cultures operate, and with the change strategies we outline later in this chapter, you'll be able to make change for yourself and others that will be sustainable.

Too Much Integration

"Ten years ago, if I was on a business trip, I'd get to my hotel in the evening, and there might be a message or two from my secretary and a couple of faxes," says Philippe Midy, a Paris-based executive at McDonald's Europe who travels extensively around the Continent dealing with supply and logistics issues. Now there's a deluge. "Sometimes I'm answering e-mails at 2 a.m.," Midy says. At least at the moment, long hours are part of the price to be paid for faster growth, especially if you work for a multinational. "If you are going to be a participant in economic activity that is part of a globalized market," notes Stephen S. Roach, chief economist for Morgan Stanley, "you need to be prepared to stretch beyond 9 to 5."

Excerpt from BusinessWeek, "The Real Reasons You're Working So Hard...and What You Can Do About It," September 22, 2005

It has gotten to the stage where Microsoft has even issued guidance to its UK employees on when they should disconnect from the Internet at home or turn off their mobile phones.

"The provision of a smart phone in no way requires users to either view or respond to business-related e-mails or calls out of office hours," Steve

Harvey, Director of People and Culture at Microsoft told CNN. "Individuals are not skilled in setting the boundaries between work and home [and] colleagues fail to respect others' rights to free time."[1]

We all know about the proliferation of cell phones, e-mail, and globalization. Yet it really is becoming a major problem that more and more people work in companies that have cultures that make them feel they can no longer "turn work off" at the end of the day. Professional responsibilities have been thoroughly integrated into personal time. But few professionals can endure extreme integration indefinitely: Eventually, they burn out. Bryan, a top consultant for McKinsey, lamented that "I never had time to think," because he was spending all his time interacting with colleagues and clients through various communication technologies. Another consultant who recently became a father reported being up at 2:00 a.m. with his new son and hearing a fax come in from a client that he knew he would have to answer by 6:00 a.m. that same day.

In companies or departments that promote too much integration between employees' professional and personal lives, managers fail to clarify when and where the employee's workday begins and ends. This failure creates what former Yale University Professor Clay Alderfer referred to as an *underbounded organization* or unit.[2] Underbounded workplaces are characterized by ambiguity, uncertainty, and mixed signals to employees about when they're on duty and when they're not. For example, a supervisor might say he respects employees' personal lives but then set a deadline that's impossible to meet by putting in a 40-hour week. Moreover, managers and employees are subjected to "fire drills" and "goat rodeos"—ulcer-causing, late-hour, all-hands-on-deck meetings called to deal with the latest crisis.

Extreme integration can spawn resentment and confusion, lead to exhaustion, and ultimately erode productivity. In some companies, loss of productivity motivates leaders to take action, as illustrated by the Microsoft vignette near the beginning of this section. But in too many underbounded organizations, managers spend so much time and energy fighting fires that they don't take steps to help employees establish boundaries between work and personal life.

For individuals who prefer to separate or volley, these kinds of workplaces can prove particularly grueling. Even for Fusion Lovers, who relish blending the many dimensions of their lives, too much integration can impose switching costs so high that integrating eventually proves impossible to maintain. Some companies or departments expect people to blend work into their personal lives to such an extent that they have little time left to attend to home and family needs. These organizations force workers to constantly walk a tightrope between their professional and personal priorities. Of course, extensive integration may be appropriate during certain periods in a person's life—such as after the birth of a baby or while caring for an elderly parent. But we believe that this way of life cannot be sustained in the long run.

Too Much Separation

Perhaps you or someone you know works in an organization or department that enforces too much separation between work and personal life—for example, by insisting on rigid work hours and forbidding personal phone calls and other interruptions during the day. In such workplaces, employees who want some degree of integration have little or no power to blend professional and personal priorities. The result? Lives that prove as unworkable as those created by forced extreme integration.

> Workers at General Motor's innovative CAMI Automotive plant, a joint venture with Suzuki, have been empowered to make decisions about how their team will complete specific tasks. Yet tight controls—such as not being able to take calls while working on the line—keep them focused solely on work throughout the day. Some team members have asked their leaders: "Why can't you see how human we are? That we need to have a break to take the occasional personal call?"[3]

Employees in these organizations or units face the longstanding problem that Harvard Business School Professor Rosabeth Moss Kanter first articulated in her classic book *Men and Women of the Corporations* (1977). In that volume, Kanter identified the "myth of separate worlds"—the widespread belief among business leaders that employees should focus solely on their professional responsibilities during the workday and ignore family or personal concerns. Managers who coerce employees to separate when they would be more productive by using some degree of integration or volleying create what scholars refer to as an *overbounded* organization or group.[4] In such workplaces, people feel torn between trying to deliver their best on the job and striving to fulfill their obligations to their families, themselves, and their communities. Overbounded organizations might establish strict policies against staff taking sick time to care for ill family members. Or they may reward people who put in "face time"—those who are present in the office all day, every day, regardless of whether their jobs require it or whether working at home might be more efficient. Hewlett-Packard, for instance, recently abolished telecommuting for nearly all IT professionals— despite rising gas prices (which suggest the wisdom of telecommuting) and advances in high-speed Internet access (which make working from home more feasible than ever).

Choosing Work or Family

Gillian Zhao, managing director of Apple China, regularly puts in 12 to 14 hour days to tackle her heavy workload. To meet targets, she must work long hours on the weekends and weekdays to stay in touch with clients and U.S. Apple executives. "Global companies have very high expectations of revenue growth in China," she says. She's glad she had her daughter (who is now 15) when she started her career as a secretary. "My job wasn't so challenging then, so I had time for a baby," she explains. The implication? If you have a challenging job, you don't have time to raise a family.

The Wall Street Journal [5]

Maybe you work in an organization or department that pushes workers to make work *or* personal and family life their top priority. The message may be tacit; for example, the company has no middle or senior managers with young families or with significant personal interests outside the office. In such work-places, managers view each of their direct reports as *career-oriented* or as *slackers*, who have sacrificed professional advancement for decades of changing diapers and carting kids to soccer practice. There is little tolerance of work-life strategies that enable people to rise in the corporate hierarchy *while also* raising families or fulfilling some other important personal objective. *Fast trackers* receive pay raises, promotions, and plum assignments—while *mommy trackers* receive nothing.

Some Work Firsters we interviewed wanted to experiment with the Quality Timer (volleying) strategy. But they worried that their bosses and colleagues would view them as not sufficiently ambitious or dedicated to their employer. Consequently, they maintained their current strategy—and risk missing out on the fulfillment and joy that a well-tended family and personal life can bring. Likewise, Firsters who made family or personal life their top priority had built a satisfying life outside work, but felt they had been excluded from the opportunities that bring fulfillment on the professional front.

Time for Change

So most employees you work with want a range of options for flexstyles, and they've started to demand more choice in the matter. But many business leaders find it much easier to manage their enterprise or work group if they apply one-size-fits-all policies to their workforces. Policies governing when, where, and how people carry out their jobs are far simpler to implement if their advocates assume that everyone works the same hours, has the same priorities, and wants to manage those priorities in the same ways. Yet in today's organization, these assumptions no longer apply.

For example, in a single department or team, some employees function best if they can separate, others if they can integrate, and still others if they can volley. Moreover, each person may possess different—and changing—degrees of control over how they manage their commitments. To illustrate, one individual who used to function productively and happily as a Fusion Lover suddenly needs to separate and make family life his top priority to take care of an elderly parent who has fallen ill. Another team member's children go off to college, giving this former Family Firster the welcome opportunity to now focus entirely on her career. Still another employee who used to keep work and home life firmly compartmentalized gets divorced and no longer has a spouse who's willing to tackle all the administrative chores that come with running a household. This person, now a Reactor, must suddenly integrate—calling the plumber or landscaper during the workday to make appointments and exchanging e-mails with the bank during the day to resolve problems with his mortgage account.

If businesses hope to retain talent, they must become flexible enough to accommodate such diversity and changes in employees' life circumstances. Effective leaders know that there is neither one best way to manage workers nor one best way for individuals to juggle their many different priorities. And they know that an approach that works for a particular person one year may no longer suit her needs the following year.

Not surprisingly, accepting these facts of business life can prove difficult for executives and managers accustomed to operating in one of the three types of problematic cultures described previously. And many such leaders may assume that more flexibility simply isn't possible in their organization or department. Nevertheless, all of us have enormous power to challenge and change the assumptions that restrict our choices about how to manage healthy work-life relationships.

Consider the widespread assumption that extreme devotion to career prevents a person from being a good parent, community member, or friend, or that putting personal life first means that an individual cannot deliver sufficient value to his employer. What if such beliefs were replaced by the (more accurate) assumption that an individual's work and personal life can actually enrich each other? For example, skills acquired on the job or at home (such as conflict resolution, time management, budgeting, and project management) can prove equally valuable in either realm. Think about it: The community leader who demonstrates talent for persuasion and project management during a major fundraising campaign brings important value to his organization when he applies these same skills at the office. Likewise, the worker who's a paragon of organization and efficiency at the office can leverage these same abilities in her personal life—whether she's managing a household, establishing a marathon training regimen, or researching retirement investment opportunities.

Most working men and women today want to succeed in every dimension of their lives. And when they do, their employers, families, and communities benefit, as do the individuals themselves. Organizations can reap their share of these benefits by transforming their cultures so that people have control over how they manage their many priorities. The payoff? A more engaged, energized, and productive workforce, which translates directly into bottom-line performance. To make this change occur, we need to have dialogue to change unhealthy organizational cultures, and we need to remove barriers to redesigning work to support schedule control over where and when one works.

Dialogue to Change Attitudes and Culture

The steps for changing attitudes and culture involve taking the initiative, modeling relationship reciprocity, modeling a healthy flexstyle, supporting equal rights for a diversity of flexstyles in productive workplaces, challenging outdated assumptions, and fostering dialogue at the top.

Take the Initiative

As the preceding discussion on unhealthy cultures demonstrates, company norms and job structures send signals to employees about which priorities the organization wants workers to have and how people are expected to manage those priorities. People watch each other at work to see who gets rewarded for which behaviors and attitudes. Then they adopt those same behaviors and attitudes to reap the benefits they've observed. For example, suppose the individuals at your company who win the most promotions, pay raises, and plum assignments are those who put in 60-hour weeks or more and who sacrifice their weekends to handle work-related emergencies. In this company, anyone interested in climbing the corporate ladder (never mind keeping her job) will feel compelled to show the same slavish devotion to the firm that the "successful" employees exhibit. And she will pay the same price in the form of a stunted personal, family, and community life, as well as the risk of eventual burnout on the job. The fear of losing one's job or missing out on opportunities for professional advancement is a strong emotion, so few people have the gumption to challenge this type of workplace culture. This means that you, as a leader, must take the initiative in fostering broad cultural change in your organization.

How to begin? Take a moment to examine the assumptions in your organization about what constitutes the "model" employee. For example, what happens to talented individuals who have expressed a desire to manage their priorities in different ways than previous top performers? Are these individuals marginalized? Valued? Heard? Ignored? Are the respect and rewards they receive commensurate with what they've contributed to the firm? Are people rewarded for managing their many priorities so as to reduce stress levels and come to work energized every day? Or are they rewarded for sacrificing their health for the company? Do high performers stay with the firm even as they begin devoting more time to their outside responsibilities? Or do they opt out of organizational life or switch to a less stressful job at a competing firm to realize their dreams of raising a family or to fulfill their responsibility to elderly parents or their community?

Many companies have traditionally rewarded Work Firsters and Captives (two types of Separators who tend to make professional life their top priority), as well as Job Warriors (who shape their family lives around the excessive workload demands of their jobs). Over time, such enterprises have grudgingly begun tolerating Fusion Lovers and Reactors, since these flexstyles emphasize responding to work demands on the spot even when employees are not in the office.

If you stand by and do nothing, you perpetuate the norms that are currently putting your firm's talent pool at risk. Or you can challenge those norms to begin crafting a culture that's more supportive of different ways of working. By taking the initiative, you help your company avoid the problems that crop up when individual managers and employees negotiate a myriad of unconnected deals. Like the vignette at the beginning of this chapter, when faced with conflicts, you can start with open dialogue with others to discuss your and their work-life needs and begin to develop a way to get the work done while at the same time respecting the personal needs of others. The example we gave is built on a norm of *relational reciprocity*.

Model Relational Reciprocity

Relational reciprocity—the exchange of support between two individuals—can enable people to forge mutually beneficial and satisfying bonds in the workplace. In the opening vignette, as a manager you can communicate to your colleague that you understand the long hours you all have been working and know how important it is to get the work done before Friday night so he can go on vacation. You can express your appreciation for the value he contributes to the company and convey a desire to help him make sure the work gets done so that he can take a well-deserved break. All these messages can tip the scale for a valued but overworked employee who's thinking about leaving the firm and going to a competitor.

To assess and strengthen your own ability to model relational reciprocity, you might ask yourself how many people you work with would agree that, first, you live a healthy flexstyle, and, second, that you have demonstrated that you are able to consider others' needs and make compromises when needed to support not only your needs but also the work-life needs of others.

Model a Healthy Flexstyle

Another way you can spur cultural change in your team or department is to model a healthy flexstyle. By living a healthy flexstyle, you have managed your own energy as a departmental resource. Writers Jim Loehr and Tony Schwartz have written about managerial engagement as a work resource in their 2003 book *The Power of Full Engagement*.[6] They suggest that each of us needs to manage our energy and not our time to promote high performance. We can nip in the bud the potential for the negative cascading impact of coworker and managerial burnout and negativity on those who work with or for us. By making sure we are managing our own energy to not become burned out, we will have more resources as a team leader to allocate to our subordinates or peers in terms of quality, quantity, focus, and emotional and spiritual engagement. So what managers need to remember to focus on is their own energy management, not just time management.

Foster Dialogue at the Top

One barrier that prevents leaders from initiating cultural change is the lack of dialogue among top executives about flexstyle issues. In many companies, the executive team has relegated work-life issues to the human resources department or benefits consultants. To be sure, these individuals can play a key role in implementing needed policies. But lack of input from senior executives on what those policies should be has resulted in "window dressing"—policies that make a workplace *seem* supportive of flexibility, without actually *being* supportive. For instance, such an organization might do the following:

- Offer a flextime policy that employees don't use because doing so only gets them ostracized by colleagues and bosses

- Give money to and participate in roundtables that examine the difficulties of managing work and nonwork priorities, without successfully implementing any solutions back at the office

- Hire a "work-life balance" consultant or full-time staffer who conducts studies but doesn't actually develop concrete, practical solutions

If your company has acquired such window dressing, your boss and colleagues may look at you quizzically when you declare the need for change. "We're already on the ball with this," they may think to themselves. Some of them might even conclude that you're an ineffective manager if you can't get your workers to use all those generous policies and resources that the company has made available.

But you know that work-life policies adopted on paper at the organizational level have little value unless they're implemented by managers at the departmental, team, and (ultimately) individual levels. When implementation is left up to managers, many of them ignore the policies because they fear retribution, or they simply don't have time to figure out how to implement them in their teams or departments. Consequently, individual managers can make or break the success of any such policy.

You must foster dialogue at the top about how your company's work-life policies are falling flat and what can be done about the situation. For example, you might point out to your executive team the problems that have come with outsourcing work-life solutions to benefits consultants. Specifically, suppose your company has purchased such services without assessing its workforce's unique needs, without discussing whether such services support its HR strategy, or without considering whether the corporate culture will accept the resulting policies. In each of these cases, the firm has probably wasted money.

Such dialogue may be particularly difficult to jump-start in boom or bust times. When business is brisk, companies feel free to spend lavishly on programs and consultants without holding program leaders and vendors accountable for the effectiveness of their services. And when times are tough, executives become reluctant to introduce policies that they view as benefiting only employees and not the company overall. For these reasons, during boom and bust periods alike, it's more important than ever that managers take the lead in promoting dialogue about how their company can support employees' efforts to construct manageable lives.

Challenge Outdated Myths About Employees' Choices

As companies have come under increasing pressure to *appear* "family friendly" or supportive of employees having lives outside work, myths have arisen to hide the fact that an organization does not *in fact* have these characteristics. For example, managers at the office say that "Mary quit because her husband was transferred and she wanted to stay home with the kids." But no one mentions that Mary—a top performer on the job—might have stayed on if she thought the firm could tolerate her working a reduced schedule or making some other change to accommodate her needs.

Consider the stories of several high-level female advisers in the George W. Bush administration. Karen Hughes and Mary Matalin quit their jobs (despite being valued members of the administration) rather than negotiating reduced working hours to fulfill family responsibilities. While this is speculation, it is possible that they believed it was easier to drop out entirely than attempt to change their organization's culture. Yet widely publicized stories in the media emphasized that each woman "wanted to spend more time with her family." These accounts made it appear that Hughes and Matalin simply left the administration when they chose to, but perhaps they saw no option other than to dropout.

Demonstrate Equal Support for Healthy Flexstyles in Productive Workplaces

We need to be careful about sending signals that seem as if we are judging or reducing coworkers' or subordinates' choices over how they manage their varied priorities. The more choices they perceive they have to be CEO of their lives and manage their flexstyles, the more in control they'll feel—and the more engaged and productive they'll be on the job.

One way to demonstrate that you care about and respect the personal needs of all the people you work with is through active behaviors. This means listening to others' needs, treating others with respect, and presenting yourself as someone with whom others can feel comfortable discussing their most important professional and personal challenges. You might ask yourself the following questions:

- Do people generally feel comfortable with me in discussing how to manage schedule conflicts yet still get the work done in time?

- Do my coworkers believe I effectively respect the personal and professional needs of everyone on our team?

- Do people see me as being able to work with others to develop strategies to enable each of us to achieve our professional and personal priorities effectively?

Equally important to changing the culture is not only informal on-the-job dialogue, but also some formal training sessions to send a signal that it is okay to talk about how to change the culture. Often questions like the preceding ones can be an ice breaker for formal training sessions. Our research has shown that this training can start with managers to help them recognize how their perceived support for work and personal lives of others is critical for others' well-being on the job. Data can be shown on how productivity is hurt—through absenteeism and turnover, for example—by not addressing work-life concerns more effectively. Then to roll out the training, workers and managers in departments are often trained to discuss how to get the work done effectively while still respecting the scheduling concerns and flexstyle preferences of team members. Once the dialogue has been started to change attitudes, norms, and culture, and to motivate group support for healthy flexstyles, you can turn to trying to make structural change. This refers to changing either the way jobs are designed or the way work processes are managed that can create barriers to supporting healthy flexstyles.

To improve work processes, treat work-life issues as a collective concern and implement change in work groups. Establish cross-training and backup systems, pilot programs, and new ways to work. We can open the books to evaluate the effectiveness of existing formal policies and work practices as barriers to change.

Improve Work Processes

Treat Work-Life Challenges as a Collective Concern
We can help change our workplaces by asking leaders and peers to view work-life challenges as a collective concern, as a collective concern that requires system-wide change to give individuals more control and accountability over the use of flexibility. Key to this approach is to establish cross-training and backup systems for each job. When you are the only go-to person on a job and there is no one to back you up, chances are you have less schedule control, particularly if you are in a job that serves customers—internal or external.

Establish Cross-Training and Backup Systems
One key approach to improving work processes is to encourage your work group to establish backup systems for each job. In other words, each person should have someone he can rely on in his absence to help get the job done in a critical time, and how every job is performed needs to be understood by at least two people. Communication mechanisms also need to be established for the tradeoff of work, and often this can be done by a company intranet or by e-mail.

So it is important to have work processes that are designed to facilitate each team member to have greater control over where, when, and how she manages work and nonwork priorities in ways that best suit her needs. For example, you might encourage your coworkers or boss to work out a plan with her team that specifies who will provide coverage during different overload times. By developing a plan that encompasses the whole group, you will help change the culture of your work group by ensuring others don't feel like deviants when they mention work/nonwork conflicts. You'll also reduce your department's dependency on one person's constant availability to continue functioning during crises.

Pilot New Ways of Working as Team Experiments and Get Feedback
One key process that can help make sure that new ways of working stick is to try out individual preferences for working and get feedback from other members to fine-tune the arrangement. This also helps you establish a sense of fairness in your team, as well as more easily orchestrate task completion throughout your group. By contrast, making one-on-one fixed

deals can have problematic consequences. For example, suppose a manager lets Bob, a Family Firster, work from home after 3:30 p.m., when his children get home from school. Bob's absence after 3:30 makes more work for Sally, a Work Firster who handles all walk-in customers and is at the office until 5:00 p.m. every day. By striking a deal with Bob, a manager creates the perception of inequity in the team.

A better solution to fix the structure would be for your team to explore piloting solutions to see how well they work for everyone. The goal is to facilitate a discussion between team members of how they can work together more effectively to get the work done with less conflict and more coordination to back each other up, and to agree to try a new way of working together on a trial basis and to collect data from each employee and client involved to see whether the system works well.

For instance, at the beginning of a group meeting, you could ask your manager to facilitate a group discussion. The meeting might begin with the statement: "Here is the work we need to get done over the next month and some typical conflicts that have come up in the past. How might we discuss new ideas for getting the workload done?" Individuals can then brainstorm, "What can we do differently to get this work done more effectively and with less conflict?" Through this discussion, you might learn that 3:30 p.m. to 5:00 p.m. is a peak time for clients to come in, but a coworker is not very busy in the morning. The co-worker offers to come in later and work during the peak time period when client demands merit this. Thus, a backup system is created.

Openly Measure the Effectiveness of Work-Life Policies

Currently, most research on work-life policies and practices is being conducted by consultants who are not associated with universities or the public sector. Thus no one is examining whether these individuals' research has generated measurable value for real-world organizations. Granted, many of these consultancies have made significant contributions to the study of work and family/personal life balance. But some of them are rewarded in ways that motivate them to focus more on getting the next contract than on being accountable for actually changing the client companies' culture and leadership systems. Internal measurement systems related to performance appraisal and rewards need to include accountability for the successful implementation of flexibility.

How do you help your company avoid wasting money on consulting advice that doesn't generate positive change? Remind leaders of the adage "What's important gets measured. What gets measured gets managed. And what gets managed gets improved." Advocate systematic evaluation of every workable-life policy's effectiveness—in terms of measurable business results. For example, has a policy recommended by a benefits consultancy noticeably reduced turnover in your firm? Has it been used by a critical mass of employees? Has it enabled workers to improve their productivity? Determine the metrics your firm might use to measure a policy's effectiveness and discuss possible actions in cases where a policy comes up short. This type of systematic assessment will quickly send the message to human resource consultancies that your firm means business—and that it won't accept policies that deliver lukewarm results.

You can help ensure that a work-life policy will deliver on its potential by suggesting that your firm take these additional actions.

Train managers and employees on how to implement the policy. For instance, if your company is experimenting with telecommuting or flextime, facilitate discussions on the importance of establishing core hours for being in the office and thinking about how to establish norms for communication when problems come up and someone is not physically at the office.

Reinforce practice of the policy with the right performance appraisal systems. For example, an employee who agrees to a reduced workload after the birth of a child should not be expected to generate the same volume of business to receive a positive performance appraisal as employees who work a full week.[7]

Align practice of flexibility policies with appropriate compensation systems. To illustrate, if someone works part of a year, payroll systems need to be updated to be flexible enough to allow for different work schedules. Some key professionals and managers we interviewed were insulted when they had to go on the nonexempt payroll when they worked a nontraditional work schedule, because the payroll system wasn't flexible enough to manage schedule diversity. When a company evaluates and takes steps to ensure the effectiveness of work-life policies, it reaps important rewards. Employees feel a greater sense of control over how they manage their many priorities. And studies show that when people feel in control of their lives, they become more loyal to their employer, their productivity increases, and they miss fewer days on the job. In addition, they feel a greater sense of commitment to their work as well as exhibit more flexibility in taking on new assignments, helping others, and making suggestions. By helping your executive team see and document these payoffs, you sweeten the odds of winning their support for diverse flexstyles.[8]

**Make the link between serving employee's needs
and serving customers needs.**

One successful tactic we saw was framing the need to support different flexstyles as not only serving employees' needs but also improving the working climate. This involves making a link between serving employees in order to better serve customers. Take the following comments made by two managers we spoke with in our research that knew the importance of making the links between responsiveness to personal needs and responsiveness to customers. They knew how to frame respecting workers personal needs as also supporting organizational effectiveness.

*To get high quality [performance], you need to be sensitive
to the personal needs that employees have.*[9]

Manager A

*A corporation's success depends on a high-quality, innovative,
and dedicated workforce. If you don't get the "people thing" right,
you won't get the "customer thing" right.*[10]

Manager B

Looking to the Future

We wrote this book to help you build satisfying professional and personal lives as well as to shape your workplaces and homes to support you in these efforts. The kinds of tools we've presented in this book—including self-reflection and dialogue with bosses, colleagues, employees, family, friends, and fellow community members—are tools we hope will help you with your journey to become the CEO of your life and to create a better working life in the flexible job age.

More and more people are trying to find new ways to create flexstyles that make them feel better about the ways their personal and professional lives fit together. And they're discovering that, to do so, we need to change the conversations we're having in our workplaces, homes, and neighborhoods. This groundswell of interest argues well for anyone seeking more creative ways to achieve a manageable and fulfilling life as well as help your colleagues and loved ones to do the same.

It is difficult (if not outright impossible) for working men and women to generate creative ideas if they're constantly mired in overfull e-mail inboxes or burned out from overwork. Likewise, people cannot care for their families, friends, and communities if they allow their professional obligations to exhaust them. By opening up the conversation to recognize the many different ways people can manage their numerous commitments—and by establishing supportive organizational cultures and work processes—we help one another construct satisfying lives within and outside the office.

If parents cannot perform their roles well, companies and the overall economy will pay the price in the effective development of the next generation of workers. For example, children may be less nurtured because parents are too burned out to interact effectively with them. Or worse yet, birth rates will keep declining in many developed countries as the best and brightest who have choices will see the joint investment in caregiving and career as just not worth the effort and tensions. By modeling healthy living in the office as well as at home, we teach that next generation of future workers to strive for the same standards when they enter adulthood.

The challenge that remains centers on how to create workplaces that welcome a variety of approaches to managing professional and personal responsibilities. Such workplaces enable each person to bring her best contributions to the table—whether that table is in the corporate conference room or the family kitchen.

Like all important efforts, the movement toward supporting a diversity of flexstyles is a work in progress. For this reason, we encourage you to apply the tools and practices offered in this book and to contact us with entirely new suggestions as well as thoughts for improving the ideas we've supplied. By experimenting with fresh approaches and freely exchanging ideas, we stand our best chance of creating a world in which people don't have to choose between excelling in their careers and excelling in their personal lives, families, and communities.

Flexstyle Web Site and Overview of Assessments

Flexstyle Web Site

We have developed a flexstyle Web site for you to go to and take online some of the assessment tools that appear in this book. You'll also find additional scales, tools, and resources. The Web site lets you know how your scores align with the individuals in the dataset and provides links to resources for change and blogs for dialoging with others. We are developing an ongoing database of participants to continue to monitor trends in scale development and healthy relationships between work and personal life.

The Web site is http://ellenkossek.lir.msu.edu

If you have any comments to share with the authors about your flexstyle or change management strategies for improving work and personal life relationships, or if you want more information on the study or scales, please contact the authors at kossek@msu.edu and blautsch@sfu.ca. The remaining sections in this Appendix include some sample qualitative and quantitative questions or topics we have used in our studies as well as sample employee, family and supervisor questions. In studying work-life relationships, it is important to have data from many different stakeholders that is both numeric and substantive.

Sample Qualitative Interview Questions

This section presents some sample questions from our employee pre-interview survey and then some follow-up interview questions we developed to ask people how they managed relationships between work and personal life.

Boundaries

I NEXT WANT TO TALK TO YOU MORE SPECIFICALLY ABOUT HOW YOU DRAW BOUNDARIES (OR DON'T) BETWEEN YOUR WORK, FAMILY, AND PERSONAL LIFE.

All in all, do you currently see yourself as someone who tries to keep work and personal roles separated most of the time or someone who tries to keep them integrated?

[1] _____Separate

[2] _____Integrate

[3] _____Neither

Please explain.

Is this your preferred strategy for managing work and personal roles?

[1] _____Yes

[2] _____No

Why or why not? Please explain.

Pros and Cons

What are the advantages of this way of managing work and family demands for you (i.e., either separating or integrating, depending on the previous answer)? What are the advantages for your work? For your family?

What are the disadvantages of this way of managing work and family demands for you? What are the disadvantages for your work? For your family?

If you separate, have you ever been unable to respond to family (or work) demands when they arise?

Have you faced any pressure from your boss or colleagues to be responsive 24/7 to work demands? If so, how have you dealt with this? Do you think your career has been influenced by your choice to separate? Please explain.

If you integrate, do you ever have trouble juggling work and family demands that arise at the same time? Is it ever confusing to know which problem to deal with first? Are your work or family times often interrupted?

Temporal Boundaries

When you work at home, do you reschedule work to attend dentist appointments or other personal or family needs?

Do you set specific work hours during the week, even when working at home?

Mental Boundaries

If working in the office, do you call home to "check-in?" How often? Or do you e-mail your children or spouse?

Do you find yourself thinking about home or personal issues while working? Do you think this happens more or less often when working at home, compared to the office?

Physical Boundaries

Can you give me examples of how you manage physical boundaries between work and personal life? Are these your preferred strategies?

Tradeoffs

Do you see any tradeoffs from these ways of working?

What are good things and bad things about boundaries?

What are some strategies you use to help you manage work and family roles? What works well and not so well?

Are there different ways your job could be organized or designed that might make it easier for you to meet your work and family obligations?

Overview of Survey Instrument

(Some or all of the following scales were used in different work-life studies we have done.)

Consent Form

Improving Employee Retention, Engagement, and Health:

Linkages to Employee Flexstyles and Work-Family-Life Effectiveness

You are being asked to participate in a study on the management of your work-life relationships in the hopes of improving your effectiveness in balancing your work and personal lives. In this study you will complete a questionnaire concerning (1) your approach to work and family boundaries; (2) how you experience work, family, and health; and (3) general demographics. The information you provide will help you identify your personal approach to work-life relationships and provide suggestions toward the management of these domains. In addition, this information will be used to guide future research in the area of work-life management. It is estimated that the survey will take about 30 minutes to complete.

Your completion of this survey is completely voluntary. You are free to not answer any question or to stop participating at any time. All questionnaires are anonymous, and the forms will be kept confidential by the researcher to the maximum extent allowable by law. There are no risks or individual benefits associated with taking this survey.

If you have any questions about this study you may call or e-mail the investigator, Professor Ellen Ernst Kossek, PhD, at (517) 353-9040, kossek@msu.edu. If you have any questions or concerns regarding your rights as a study participant, you may contact your local university's Human Subject Protection Department.

By completing this survey, you indicate your voluntary consent to participate in this study and have your answers included in the project dataset.

Part I: Identifying Your Overall Flexstyle Category (See assessment at end of Chapter 2.)

Part II: Tradeoffs and Effectiveness of Specific Flexstyles

Integrator Flexstyle Tradeoffs (See full assessment at end of Chapter 4.)

A. If You're a Reactor; Section B.
   Sample Item: *I am less effective than I could be because I am constantly switching back and forth between work and family.*

B. If You're a Fusion Lover.
   Sample Item: *I am not sure if my way of multitasking is sustainable over the long run in my life.*

Separator Flexstyle Tradeoffs (See full assessment at end of Chapter 5.)

A. If You're a Firster (Work or Family); B.
   Sample Item: *Reflecting back over the last six months, I can think of numerous times when I wished I had more time or energy to devote to my (choose one that you are sacrificing nonwork/work) life.*

B. If You're a Captive.
   Sample Item: *I must find a more flexible way to manage work and personal life.*

Volleyers Flexstyle Tradeoffs (See full assessment at end of Chapter 6.)

A. If You're a Quality Timer; B.
   Sample Item: *I would like to explore new ways of improving how I am balancing work and personal life.*

B. If You're a Job Warrior.
   Sample Item: *My family sometimes doesn't understand that I need time just to relax when I get back from working on a major job project or a business trip.*

Part III: Work–Life Flexibility Satisfaction and Psychological Job Control Assessment

Scale Info
Work Life Satisfaction Scale (For full scale, see Valcour, M. (In Press, 2007). Work-based Resources as Moderators of the Relationship between Work Hours and Satisfaction with Work-family Balance. *Journal of Applied Psychology.*

Sample Item: *How satisfied are you with how well your work life and your personal or family life fit together?*

Personal Flexibility Control (For full scale, see Kossek, E., Lautsch, B., Eaton, S. 2006. Telecommuting, control, and boundary management: Correlates of policy use and practice, job control, and work-family effectiveness. *Journal of Vocational Behavior, 68,* 347-367.

Sample Items: *To what extent does your job permit you to decide on your own about WHERE the work is done?*

To what extent does your job permit you to decide about WHEN the work is done?

Part IV: General Health and Well-Being; Alcohol and Tobacco Use

Depressive Symptoms
Sample Item: *How often have you experienced each of these during the past month? (1) You felt cheerful.*

Part V. Supervisor Satisfaction with Style

Sample Item: *My supervisor generally prefers, and is more satisfied, when I make work my top priority.*

Part VI. Family Satisfaction with Style

Sample Item: *My family generally prefers, and is more satisfied, when I make family my top priority.*

Part VII. Personal Characteristics and Context
- Personality
- Job characteristics and control
- Job satisfaction
- Family flexibility
- Work and family resources
- Social support

Part VIII. Outcomes
- Work-family Conflict
- Work-family enrichment and engagement
- Satisfaction with work-family balance
- Job and life, family/marital satisfaction
- Job performance
- Family performance
- Intent to turnover
- Depressive symptoms
- General health and well-being

Part IX: Getting Input from Those Who Know You: Your Supervisor and Family

Sample Item: *I am generally satisfied with how XXXX(insert your name) manages work and family relationships.*

Part X: Demographics

Quiz

> The following questions will help us to describe the participants in the study in general terms but will never be used to identify you personally. It helps support the credibility of the study to discuss the sample in general terms.

1. What is your official job title? (please spell out)_____

2. What company do you work for?_____

3. How long have you worked for this company?_____Years   _____Months

4. Do you work?
   - ☐ Full time
   - ☐ Part time

5. On average, in this job, how many **hours** do you actually work **per week?** _____ hours

6. On average, in this job, how many **days** do you actually work **per week?** _____ days

7. Would you prefer to work more, fewer or the same number of **hours?**
   - ☐ More
   - ☐ Fewer
   - ☐ The same

8. Would you prefer to work more, fewer or the same number of **days?**
   - ☐ More
   - ☐ Fewer
   - ☐ The Same

9. Do you currently use any of the following:

   a. Flextime (control of work schedule starting and stopping time)
   - ☐ yes
   - ☐ no

   b. Telecommute (work from home office)
   - ☐ yes
   - ☐ no

   c. Part time or reduced load work that is less than full time
     ☐ yes
     ☐ no

   d. Check email or do other work on before or after regular working hours
     ☐ yes
     ☐ no

   e. Work during a week of vacation
     ☐ yes
     ☐ no

   f. Work when sick in a week
     ☐ yes
     ☐ no

If yes to any of the above, please indicate how many days in a typical week from one to seven days you used these forms of flexibility:

10. Flextime_____days

11. Telecommute_____days

12. Part time or reduced load work_____days

13. Check email or do other work before or after regular work hours_____days

14. Work during a week of vacation_____days

15. Work when sick in a week_____days

16. What is your age?_____

17. What is your gender?
   ☐ Male
   ☐ Female

18. What is your race? (check all that apply)
   ☐ White
   ☐ Black or African American
   ☐ American Indian or Alaskan native
   ☐ Asian
   ☐ Native Hawaiian or other Pacific Islander
   ☐ Other_____

19. Are you Hispanic or Latino/Latina?
   ☐ Yes
   ☐ No

20. If yes, are you:
    ☐ Mexican American, Chicano
    ☐ Cuban
    ☐ Puerto Rican
    ☐ Central American
    ☐ South American
    ☐ Other_____

21. Were you born in the United States? (If yes, skip to next **Question 25**)
    ☐ Yes
    ☐ No

22. If no, where were you born?_____

23. At what age did you come to the US? _____years

24. How many years have you lived in the United States continuously? _____years

25. What is the highest level of education you have completed?
    ☐ Some high school
    ☐ High school diploma or GED
    ☐ Some college or associate's degree
    ☐ Bachelor's degree
    ☐ Graduate degree

26. What is your commute time to work in one direction?_____hours   _____minutes

27. Which of the following statements describes your ability to get along on your income?
    ☐ We can't make ends meet
    ☐ We have just enough, no more
    ☐ We have enough, with a little extra, sometimes
    ☐ We always have money left over

28. What was your total household income in the past 12 months?
    ☐ Less than $25,000
    ☐ $25,000-$40,000
    ☐ $40,000-$55,000
    ☐ $55,000-$70,000
    ☐ $80,000-$85,000
    ☐ Over $85,000

29. Please list the ages of your children: 1) _____ years   2) _____ years
                                          3) _____ years   4) _____ years

30. Do you provide care for adults or elders.
    ☐ Yes
    ☐ No

If yes please explain_____

We also often interview supervisors of employees to understand their approach to manage flexibility and the work and family demands of subordinates. Below are some sample survey items.

Sample Manager Survey Questions

Would you describe you organization as family-friendly?	☐ Not at all ☐ Somewhat unfriendly ☐ Neither friendly nor unfriendly ☐ Somewhat friendly ☐ Very friendly
In responding to the following statements, indicate whether you:	☐ Strongly disagree ☐ Disagree ☐ Neither agree nor disagree ☐ Agree ☐ Strongly agree
When employees have personal issues, I wish they would leave them at home.	☐ Strongly disagree ☐ Disagree ☐ Neither agree nor disagree ☐ Agree ☐ Strongly agree
I am willing to help fill in for employees when they have personal problems.	☐ Strongly disagree ☐ Disagree ☐ Neither agree nor disagree ☐ Agree ☐ Strongly agree
I am satisfied with the way my organization handles work-family conflict	☐ Strongly disagree ☐ Disagre ☐ Neither agree nor disagree ☐ Agree ☐ Strongly agree
I experience a lot of stress as a supervisor.	☐ Strongly disagree ☐ Disagree ☐ Neither agree nor disagree ☐ Agree ☐ Strongly agree
Use of flexible arrangements such as telecommuting by employees increases the difficulty of my job supervising them.	☐ Strongly disagree ☐ Disagree ☐ Neither agree nor disagree ☐ Agree ☐ Strongly agree
I would like to do more telecommuting myself.	☐ Strongly disagree ☐ Disagree ☐ Neither agree nor disagree ☐ Agree ☐ Strongly agree

Sample Manager Survey Questions (continued)

I am generally a person who keeps work and home issues separate.	☐ Strongly disagree ☐ Disagree ☐ Neither agree nor disagree ☐ Agree ☐ Strongly agree
I am willing to adjust work schedules so employees can take care of family needs.	☐ Strongly disagree ☐ Disagree ☐ Neither agree nor disagree ☐ Agree ☐ Strongly agree
I believe people who spend a lot of time at work are more productive.	☐ Strongly disagree ☐ Disagree ☐ Neither agree nor disagree ☐ Agree ☐ Strongly agree
What have you learned from your experience about how best to manage employees using flexible work policies (e.g., telecommuters?)	Text
What kinds of jobs work best for use of flexibility (e.g. telecommuting?)	Text
Do you feel that you have enough authority over employees working flexibly? (e.g., telecommuters)	☐ Yes ☐ No

Notes

Chapter 1

1. Mary isn't alone in this. For more information on how few people are taking real vacations, see Timothy Egan, "The Rise of the Shrinking Vacation," *New York Times* PA18(L) (August 20, 2006): 1.

2. See, for example, D.M. Rousseau, *Psychological Contracts in Organizations; Understanding Written and Unwritten Agreements* (Thousand Oaks, CA: Sage, 1995).

3. For helpful analysis of U.S. Census Bureau statistics see Bianchi, S. & Raley, S. (2005) Time allocation in families In Work, Family Health and Well-being. (Bianchi, S., Casper, L. & King, R.) NY: Routledge, pp. 21–42.

4. Herminia Ibarra, (2003) *Working Identity: Unconventional Strategies for Reinventing Your Career.* Boston: Harvard Business School Publishing.

Chapter 2

1. Interested readers may also want to refer to Christine Nippert-Eng's wonderful ethnographic book on managing boundaries entitled: *Home and Work* (Chicago: University of Chicago Press, 1996).

Chapter 4

1. Van Dyne, L., & Ellis, J.B. (2004). Job creep :A reactance theory perspective on organizational citizenship behavior as over-fulfillment of obligations. In J. A.M. Coyle-Shapiro, L. M. Shore, M. S. Taylor, & L. E. Tetrick (Eds.), The employment relationship: Examining

psychological and contextual perspectives (p.p. 181–205). Oxford, UK: Oxford University Press.

2. For a discussion of transitions in role identities see Ashforth, B. (2001) *Role Transitions in Organizational Life: An Identity-based Perspective*, Rahway, New Jersey: LEA Press (Now Taylor and Francis).

3. Mandy van der Velde and Jan A. Fejj, "Change of Work Perceptions and Work Outcomes as a Result of Voluntary and Involuntary Job Change," *Journal of Occupational and Organizational Psychology* 68(4): 273–90; Linn Van Dyne and Soon Ang, "Organizational Citizenship Behavior of Contingent Workers in Singapore," *Academy of Management Journal* 51:692–703.

Chapter 5

1. For a discussion of work-family enrichment see, for example, Greenhaus, J. & Powell, G. 2006. When work and family are allies: A theory of work-family enrichment. *Academy of Management Review*, 31(1) 72–92.

2. See, for example, MIT Professor Lotte Bailyn's book, Breaking the mold. NY: Basic Books, 1993.

Chapter 7

1. See, for example, Lewin's influential (1951) model of change which describes change beginning with "unfreezing" behavior and developing an acceptance of the need to change. (*Field Theory in Social Science*, Harper and Row, New York, N.Y.)

2. Snyder, M., Gangestad, S. 1986. On the nature of self–monitoring: Matters of assessment, matters of validity. *Journal of Personality and Social Psychology*. Jul;51(1):125–39.

3. Those interested in goal setting might want to read E. A. Locke and G. P. Latham, *A Theory of Goal Setting and Task Performance*; (Englewood Cliffs, NJ: Prentice Hall, 1990).

4. Peter M. Senge, *The Fifth Discipline* (New York: Currency Doubleday, 1990).

5. For more information on the concept that telling someone about good news increases the positive psychological effects see Gable, S., Reiss, H., Impett, E., Asher, E. 2004. What do you do when things go right? The intrapersonal and interpersonal benefits of sharing positive events. *Journal of Personality and Social Psychology.* 87(2): 228–245.

6. Retrieved from www.creatingminds.org/quotes/change.htm.

7. Pamela Kruger, "Jobs for Life," *Fastcompany.com* 34 (April 2000): 236, http://www.fastcompany.com/magazine/34/ernst.html.

Chapter 8

1. Westman, M., Etzion, D. and Gortler, E. 2004. The work–family interface and burnout. International Journal of Stress Management. 11 (4) 413–428.

2. Zoe I. Barsness, Kristina A. Diekmann, and Marc-David L. Seidel, "Motivation and Opportunity: The Role of Remote Work, Demographic Dissimilarity, and Social Network Centrality in Impression Management," *Academy of Management Journal* 48, no. 3: 401–19.

3. Debra L. Nelson, "Women Executives: Health, Stress, and Success," *Academy of Management Executive* 14, no. 2 (May 2000): p107, 15p, 2bw.

4. Professor Blake Ashforth has raised this strategy in some of his writings on boundary management.

5. Susanne Tietze, "When 'Work' Comes 'Home': Coping Strategies of Teleworkers and Their Families," *Journal of Business Ethics* 41 (2002): 385–96.

Chapter 9

1. A. O. Hirschman, Exit, Voice and Loyalty (Cambridge: Harvard University Press, 1970); M. J. Withey and W. H. Cooper, "Predicting Exit, Voice, Loyalty, and Neglect" *Administrative Science Quarterly* 34 (1989): 521–39.

2. J. Z. Rubin and B. Brown, *The Social Psychology of Bargaining and Negotiation* (New York: Academic Press, 1975).

3. J. Rubin, some wise and mistaken assumptions about conflict and negotiation in D. Ancona, T. Kochan, M. Scully, J. Van Manann, and E. Westney, *Organizational Behavior and Processes* (Santa Fe: Southwestern Publishing, 1999): M–12, 24–31.

4. Richard E. Walton and Robert B. McKersie, A Behavioral Theory of Labor Negotiations: An Analysis of a Social Interaction System (New York: McGraw-Hill, 1965).

5. Roger Fisher and William Ury, *Getting to Yes: Negotiating Agreement Without Giving In*, (New York: Penguin Books, 1983).

6. Jane Dutton, Regina O'Neill, and Katherine Lawrence, "Moves That Matter: Issue Selling and Organizational Change," *Academy of Management Journal*, 44, no. 4: 716–36.

7. Susanne Tietze, "When 'Work' Comes 'Home': Coping Strategies of Teleworkers and Their Families," *Journal of Business Ethics* 41 (2002): 385–96.

8. *Ibid.*, 392–93.

9. *Ibid.*, 390.

10. J. W. Schulz and D. G. Pruitt, "The Effects of Mutual Concern on Joint Welfare," *Journal of Experimental Social Psychology* 14 (1977): 480–92; D. W. Schoeninger and W. D. Wood, "Comparison of Married and Ad Hoc Mixed-Sex Dyads Negotiating the Division of a Reward," *Journal of Experimental Social Psychology* 5 (1969): 483–99; P. J. Carnevale and D. G. Pruitt, "Negotiation and Mediation," *Annual Review of Psychology* 43 (1992): 531–82.

Chapter 10

1. http://edition.cnn.com/2004/BUSINESS/04/13/go.work.life.tech/index.html.

2. Alderfer, C.P. 1980. Consulting to underbounded systems. In C.P. Alderfer & C.L. Cooper (Eds.) Advances in experiential social processes (Vol. 2, pp 267–295). New York: John Wiley.

3. Canadian Auto Workers, "Working Lean." 1993. Video

4. Kanter, R. M. 1983 Men and Women of the Corporation. NY Basic Books.

5. Carol Hymowitz, "Chinese Women Bosses: Long Hours Don't Hurt Kids," *The Wall Street Journal*, May 17, 2005.

6. See Jim Loher and Tony Schwartz (2003) The Power of Full Engagement NY: Simon and Schuster.

7. E. Kossek and M. Lee, "Making Flexibility Work: What Managers Have Learned About Implementing Reduced Load Work," published online at http://flex-work.lir.msu.edu/.

8. Roehling, P.V., Roehling, M.V., & Moen, P. (2001). The relationship between work-life policies and practices and employee loyalty: a life course perspective. *Journal of Family and Economic Issues*, 22, 141–170; Konrad and Mangel 2000. *The Impact of Work-Life Programs on Firm Productivity*. By: Konrad, Alison M.; Mangel, Robert. Strategic Management Journal, Dec. 2000, Vol. 21 Issue 12, p1225, 14p; *The Impact of Flexible Scheduling on Employee Attendance and Turnover.* Dalton, Dan R.; Mesch, Debra J.. Administrative Science Quarterly, June 1990, Vol. 35 Issue 2, pgs. 370–387, 18p; Grover, S. & Crooker, K. (1995). Who appreciates family-responsive human resource policies: The impact of family-friendly policies on the organizational attachment of parents and non-parents. *Personnel Psychology*, 48: 271–288 Lambert 2000. Lambert, S. (2000). Added benefits: The Link Between Work-Life Benefits and Organizational Citizenship Behavior. *Academy of Management Journal*, 43: 801–815.

9. Kossek, E. Support of work/life integration: Cultural issues facing the employer. In E. Kossek & R. Block. Managing Human Resources in the 21st century: From core concepts to strategic choice. Cincinnati: Southwestern Publishing, ppp.11.1–11.22 (2000).

10. *Ibid.*

UU Wharton School Publishing

In the face of accelerating turbulence and change, business leaders and policy makers need new ways of thinking to sustain performance and growth.

Wharton School Publishing offers a trusted source for stimulating ideas from thought leaders who provide new mental models to address changes in strategy, management, and finance. We seek out authors from diverse disciplines with a profound understanding of change and its implications. We offer books and tools that help executives respond to the challenge of change.

Every book and management tool we publish meets quality standards set by The Wharton School of the University of Pennsylvania. Each title is reviewed by the Wharton School Publishing Editorial Board before being given Wharton's seal of approval. This ensures that Wharton publications are timely, relevant, important, conceptually sound or empirically based, and implementable.

To fit our readers' learning preferences, Wharton publications are available in multiple formats, including books, audio, and electronic.

To find out more about our books and management tools, visit us at whartonsp.com and Wharton's executive education site, exceed.wharton.upenn.edu.

Four Secrets to Liking Your Work
You May Not Need to Quit to Get the Job You Want

EDWARD G. MUZIO, DEBORAH J. FISHER, PHD, AND ERV THOMAS, PE

How far could you go if you truly loved your job? How much money could you make? How much could you learn? What could you contribute to the world, your family, yourself? Imagine living and working like this for a lifetime...now, make it happen, with *Four Secrets to Liking Your Work*! This book is not a "stop-whining-fast" program: it's about what you can do to improve your worklife, one day at a time, starting right now. Based on the latest research, it brings together state-of-the-art tools, hands-on exercises, and insights everyone can use—whatever your situation, skills, workplace, or goals. You'll begin by discovering a radically new outlook on your job: one that helps you respond to your current situation far more productively. Next, understand hidden differences in focus and approach that shape your behavior; and learn how to achieve better outcomes with far less stress. Clarify what really motivates you and your colleagues: then, use that knowledge to improve your interactions, increase your influence, and align your work with what you care about most. Learn how to "balance" your tasks, so you consistently get the positive feedback you need to move forward. Identify specific skills that can impact your effectiveness most powerfully, and master them as rapidly as possible. Finally, bring together everything you've learned, gaining a broader perspective that helps you systematically uncover obstacles to worklife satisfaction...and overcome them!

ISBN 9780132344456, © 2008, 176 pp., $18.99 USA, $20.99 CAN

Success Built to Last
Creating a Life that Matters

JERRY PORRAS, STEWART EMERY, AND MARK THOMPSON

Imagine meeting more than 300 people who've made a profound difference: not for weeks or months, but for decades. Imagine discovering what they've got in common, distilling it into a set of simple practices, and using them to transform your life. You've just imagined *Success Built to Last*. Authored by three legends in leadership and self-help, including *Built to Last* co-author Jerry Porras, it challenges conventional wisdom at every step. You'll meet world-renowned leaders like Nelson Mandela and Charles Schwab, but you'll also meet unsung heroes who've achieved lasting greatness without obvious power or charisma. Famous or not, they all started out ordinary. You'll discover how they learned how to "harvest" their strengths and their weaknesses, their victories and their surprising failures. You'll learn how they found meaning, and the courage to follow their passions. Above all, you'll see how they've sustained success. If you're a leader, this book is your true "prequel" to *Built to Last*, your personal foundation for building organizations that stay great. Whatever your goals, it will help you magnify your lifetime impact and gain the deep fulfillment of a life well-lived.

ISBN 9780132287517, © 2007, 304 pp., $22.99 USA, $25.99 CAN